PRISONERS
OF THE KAISER

PRISONERS OF THE KAISER

The last POWs of the Great War

Richard van Emden

Based on the Channel Four documentary

Pen & Sword
MILITARY

First published in Great Britain in 2009 by
Pen & Sword Military
an imprint of
Pen & Sword Books Ltd
47 Church Street
Barnsley
South Yorkshire
S70 2AS

ISBN 978 1 848840 78 2

A CIP catalogue record for this book is
available from the British Library

Typeset in Palatino by
Phoenix Typesetting, Auldgirth, Dumfriesshire

Printed and bound in England by CPI UK

Pen & Sword Books Ltd incorporates the Imprints of Pen & Sword Aviation,
Pen & Sword Maritime, Pen & Sword Military, Wharncliffe Local History,
Pen & Sword Select, Pen & Sword Military Classics and Leo Cooper.

For a complete list of Pen & Sword titles please contact
PEN & SWORD BOOKS LIMITED
47 Church Street, Barnsley, South Yorkshire, S70 2AS, England
E-mail: enquiries@pen-and-sword.co.uk
Website: www.pen-and-sword.co.uk

CONTENTS

ACKNOWLEDGEMENTS

I should like to thank all those who have supported me while I have been writing this book, particularly Steve Humphries, Director of Testimony Films, who has allowed me to take time out from work to research and write Prisoners of the Kaiser. I would also like to thank others at Testimony Films for their encouragement and help, particularly Elke Mund-Amos, Andy Attenburrow and Mathilde Damoisel but also Katherine Nightingale, and Nick Maddocks.

Many thanks also go to Roni and Paul Wilkinson who never fail to hit the tight deadlines they are given to turn round the books, and to Henry Wilson, Charles Hewitt and Paula Hurst for believing in the books that I am writing.

A very big thank you must go to my parents, Joan and Wolfgang van Emden, whose efficient editing has ensured, once again, that infinitives are not split, and that commas are in all the right places. Their help has been invaluable.

I would also like to thank the following at Channel Four: Tim Gardam Director of Programmes, Janice Hadlow, Head of History, Tim Kirby, Series Editor of the Secret History strand.

Further thanks go to: Anna van Emden, Mike Pharey, Peter Barton, Klaus Otte, Dennis Goodwin, Sanjeev Ahuja and a special thanks to Lawrence Brown for supplying the cover image.

Finally, I would like to thank all those who kindly contacted me with offers of help, including the loan of precious photographs and documents. The list is long, but I would particularly like to thank Jonathan Adams, Kevin Hoyland, Rita Schofield, Tom Donovan, as well as Tony Allen, Jean-Claude Fombaron, Adrian Dixon, Leonard Woods, and the Museum of The Prince of Wales' Own Regiment of Yorkshire.

And very lastly, thank you to all the veterans whose memories of their time as prisoners of war have been both illuminating and gripping. I hope this book is a fitting tribute to your courage and endurance.

PICTURE CREDITS

The author and publisher would like to acknowledge the following for their permission to reproduce the photographs:
The Imperial War Museum
The Taylor Library
David Bilton
The Trustees of the Manchester Regiment

This book is dedicated to the last known surviving British prisoners of war who was captured during the First World War

Pte Harold Lawton No41648
27th July 1899 – 23rd December 2005
1/4th East Yorkshire Regiment

And to the other 21 British prisoners known to be alive at the inception of this project, 1st January 1999

Lt James Anderson
7th September 1899 – 10th July 1999
101 Squadron Royal Flying Corps

Cpl Norman Cowan No42843
5th October 1898 –26th February 2002
A Squ. Northumberland Hussars

Pte Sidney Beer No57394
13th August 1898 – February 2001
2nd Middlesex Regiment

Pte Frank Deane No91675
18th February 1899 – 28th October 2002
1/6th Durham Light Infantry

Temp. 2/Lt Thomas Cavanagh
28th January 1898 – 6th January 1999
1/5th Yorkshire Regiment

Pte William Easton No2443
15th October 1898 – 18th August 1999
77th Field Ambulance RAMC

Sgt Joseph Fitzpatrick No251043
25 Dec. 1895 – 22nd April 1999
2/6th Manchester Regiment

Pte Alfred Putnam No69643
5th Dec. 1898 – 26th Sept. 1999
17th (City of London) Royal Fusiliers

L/Cpl Vincent Foulkes No52822
25th July 1899 – 16th August 2001
1/4th East Yorkshire Regiment

Pte Jack Rogers No267760
21st March 1894 – 13th April 2000
1/7th Sherwood Foresters

Pte George Gadsby No21705
4th March 1898 – 8th April 2000
1/18th (Irish Rifles) London Rgt.

Pte Thomas Spriggs No103938
2nd July 1897 – 31st January 2001
55th Division Machine Gun Corps

Pte Tommy Gay No20478
25th April 1898 – 19th February 1999
2nd Royal Scots Fusiliers

L/Cpl Ernie Stevens No54122
26th July 1899 – 29th November 1999
20th Middlesex Regiment

Pte Frederick Hammond No325027
27th Sept. 1897 – 18th April 1999
1/8th Lancashire Fusiliers

Pte Sidney White No90080
31st May 1899 – 25th January 2000
2/4th London Regiment

Pte Walter Humphrys No523990
5th September 1897 – 17th April 2003
1/15th (Civil Service Rifles) London Rgt.

Pte Percy Williams No75273
15th September 1899 – 28th May 2000
1/5th Northumberland Fusiliers

Pte John Keiller No43355
10th March 1897 – 18th August 2001
17th Highland Light Infantry

Pte Alfred Wood No41913
29th December 1898 – 5th July 1999
6th Leicestershire Regiment

Pte Richard Mills No35496
5th July 1899 – 24th April 1999
2nd West Yorkshire Regiment

Introduction

The men whose stories are told in this book were remarkable, their recollections a final testament to a time in history almost beyond human recall. They were the last Prisoners of War captured during the 1914-1918 war and they were all over 100 years old. The search for these men was exhaustive, and they represented almost all the surviving British prisoners at that time. Sadly, even as I wrote, they faded away. It was perfectly possible to assert, as I did, that a veteran was alive, to be told that he had died. He was alive in my mind because I had recently photographed him, and although frailer than when I first met him, he was as mentally active as ever. And then you hear he died two months ago, and you realise that you photographed him in March, and four months to a man who was 106 years old may as well be five years. Such was the case with former PoW Jack Rogers, a man I will always remember as affable, gentlemanly, courteous and kind.

If there was a common thread in the stories of all those captured during the First World War, it is that they never expected to become prisoners of war. For the nature of conflict at the front brought on a particular fatalism, perhaps unique to this War. The soldiers who went abroad to serve fully expected to fight, and most expected to at least be wounded in action. All – no doubt – harboured the desire to come back alive and whole, but short of that, they desired either a quick and merciful death or an injury that would send them home, light enough not to blight their lives but harsh enough to preclude any further participation in the war. None of the men I met during the research for this book ever expected to be taken prisoner. Their capture was a surprise. Then it was a shock.

Given the close proximity of the enemy, this may seem

surprising. In the world of trench warfare, when attacks and counter attacks were common, capture, while not a probability, was nevertheless a distinct possibility. In such extremes, soldiers who were cut off with no possible means of escape had only two options, to fight to the death or surrender. Most chose surrender. Only on rare occasions were men expected to fight to the bitter end and even then, when ammunition had run out, not even the most hardened of officers or NCOs could expect a man to forfeit his life for no further gain. Nevertheless, many soldiers expressed shame or disgust at having to surrender, as if the act in itself was proof of a lack of moral fibre or, worse still, outright cowardice.

Statistically, the vast majority of soldiers were, as one might expect, never taken prisoner. While 50 per cent of all those who served could expect to be killed or wounded, only around 2.8 per cent, or approximately 170,000 British servicemen, were captured on the Western Front, over half of these being taken prisoner only during the last eight months of the war. Set against this number the grim figure that two million men were wounded and around one million killed, and there is apparently ample reason to explain why capture came as such a surprise.

Yet statistics alone do not give the whole picture. The soldier's surprise at capture was as much sociological as it was statistical, being bound up partly in the way men were brought up to see themselves. From the time schoolchildren were taught the dates of innumerable British battlefield victories, boys, in particular, were infused with the history and the glory of Empire. Any defeats were glorious because of the apparent self-sacrifice of the defenders, narrow victories were won through the determination of the thin red line not to give in or give way. Surrender, though it occurred more often that it was polite to mention, was politically not on the agenda. Young lads were brought up with the "Boy's Own" interpretation of warfare and no one was there to refute that idea. There was no great legion of veterans to tell alternative stories of warfare, and no bomb damage to show the consequences of fighting. The last significant engagement had been the Boer War, when, despite failures, Britain had still won through. Defeats such as Spion Kop were immortalised for their heroism, and reliefs, such as at Kimberley and Mafeking, were characterised by their steadfastness and their very unwillingness to surrender.

When these boys joined up for the First World War, the last thing on their or anyone else's minds was the notion of surrender. Training was tough and, for the majority, thorough. The Kitchener recruits typically had a year's training before they saw action overseas. Few, if any, were ever taught what to do in the event of being cut off and surrounded other than to fight their way out. What to do in the event of capture was couched in terms not of how best to surrender in order to survive but in terms of how, once caught, one might cause the enemy as much trouble as possible. Escape of course was the ultimate aim.

As school history taught no lessons on surrender, so the army used regimental tradition and honour to reinforce the notions of what was proper and right. If those going to the front did not imagine themselves performing great heroics (and some no doubt did for a while) then they certainly expected to do their duty to King and Country. In part, this meant trying not to bring dishonour to the regiment, but most of all it meant standing true with your pals, through thick and thin.

There were pressures on officers and men not to surrender, but less so than one might imagine, as few conceived of such an eventuality. However, after their imprisonment many officers were asked to write accounts of their capture, explaining the exact circumstances by which they came to surrender. Quite clearly, there was an air of suspicion attached to capture that was missing from most cases of personal injury or death. Did the army foster this climate of mild suspicion to ensure that officers kept to the highest traditions or did they undertake enquiries in order to guard against an officer's reputation being unduly impugned? Who knows? What is certain is that many officers were happy to write such reports, in the aftermath of which they received a letter exonerating them of any blame. No such reports were asked of the ordinary ranks, not least because, as they were under orders, the precise circumstances of their capture would not have been of their making.

My interest in the plight and fate of prisoners of war was sparked by a minor comment made in a book somewhat removed from the POWs' story. In the preamble to *The Occupation of the Rhineland*, by the noted historian Sir James Edmonds, reference is made to the return of POWs to British lines as part of the Armistice requirements. On page 51, he writes that 'On 9th January 1919, the Commission reported a discrepancy of over 22,000 in the count of prisoners. By the British records there should have been about 36,000 still in the hands of the Germans, but they insisted that the total was only 13,579.' While stories about the prisoners of the Second World War are familiar to most, far less is known about POW life during the First World War. Edmonds' 'discrepancy' began a search to discover more about what had happened, through the stories of the last survivors.

The challenge was considerable, not least because statistically I could expect to find fewer then three POWs for every 100 First World War veterans contacted. As veterans were few on the ground in any case, probably under 1500 nationally at the beginning of the research project (nominally 1st January 1999), it was a potentially fruitless cause. From previous interviews over the years, I knew of four surviving POWs, but to write a book I would need a greater number and a broader cross-section of experience.

Letters, advertisements, contacts within the First War 'industry' and a newspaper article elicited 19 former POWs with an average age, at the time, of just over 101 years. When first contacted, six were still living in their homes, while the rest lived in nursing homes and sheltered accommodation. Apart from two who lived abroad, the remaining 17 veterans came from across Britain, from as far afield as the Isle of Wight, Newcastle upon Tyne, Lincoln, Cumbria, Leicester, London, Manchester and Kings Lynn. Three more prisoners were subsequently discovered in the years after this book was written.

All had dates of birth in the century before last. The youngest was then 101, the oldest 106. Of these 19, two died before contact could be made and a further eight were either too ill to be interviewed or had memories which had faded too much in recent years. One veteran, George Gadsby, had, however, written his memoirs shortly after the war and, with his and his daughter's blessing, extended extracts have been included in this book. This left 10 POWs whose memories, as I discovered, were remarkable, often moving and certainly vivid. It is their stories that form the basis of this book, but it is dedicated to all those remarkable men.

As I have almost always found with veterans of the First World War, these old soldiers were more than willing to help with this undertaking. Perhaps time had helped soften some of the more traumatic memories, but on the whole I believe that there was a sea change in attitudes by men who thirty or forty years ago would not have been willing to recall the events of more than forty years earlier. Now, so late in their lives, they were not just able but willing to tell of what happened, in the knowledge that unless they spoke then their voice would never be heard. It is not hard to imagine what a privilege it was to be the recipient of these stories, knowing that in many cases they had never been told before.

Patient and tolerant, these veterans spent many hours telling their stories. In two cases, memories were almost photographic; the rest slowly but surely pieced their recollections together. Old pictures were found, worn documents pulled from desks or drawers while memories were racked for details that to the veterans must have seemed at times inconsequential.

After the First World War, a number of memoirs were published, written by former POWs chronicling, in the writing style of the time, life behind barbed wire. After this, there was an almost total silence save for a couple of books in the 1980s that drew on diary extracts kept at the Imperial War Museum. After the mid eighties, interest in the First World War burgeoned, but while books were written on almost every aspect of the war imaginable, the POW was sidelined.

This book does not claim to cover all aspects of the prisoner of war ex-perience. Of the interviews featured, all are of privates and junior NCOs; sadly none are of officers. Nor does this book cover the war in its entirety. Numerically, few prisoners were taken in 1915 and 1916, the vast majority being captured in 1917 and 1918, during German offensives or counter offensives, and my interviews reflected this. Of the 20,000 men who were captured in 1914, there were none left. The entire generation of soldiers who fought at Mons, Le Cateau and First Ypres had gone, the last two POWs from that era both dying in the late 1990s.

The stories contained in this book are nevertheless remark-able. Powerful recollections of capture or escape are more important than to whom, where, or in what year they occurred. For a man standing with a bayonet tip at his stomach, or an escapee dashing across a field at night, there is a primitive fear regardless of whether he wears pips on his shoulders or stripes on his arm.

Each chapter in the book takes the reader through an aspect of the POW experience as it mattered most to the prisoner himself: capture, the transportation to Germany, camp life, the agony of hunger, the importance of Red Cross support for survival, and finally the joy of release. These were themes common to all prisoners, and their stories are placed into context by a narrative that draws on the greater military, social and political themes of the time. To illustrate the book, a large number of images and illustrations were drawn together. Many belonged to the veterans themselves, others came from public and private collections. Few have ever been published before. It is, I hope, a lasting tribute to that generation.

Richard van Emden
1st February 2009

CHAPTER ONE

The Moment of Capture

The transition from soldier to prisoner has always been a precarious one. History is littered with evidence of POWs being maltreated and even killed, and no amount of legislation, national or international, has guaranteed survival, or ever will do. The bitterer the war, the harder it is to hand over a weapon to an enemy who, from that time onwards, will be the arbiter over life or death. Surviving that moment will depend on a multitude of factors that few soldiers would be able to predict, and fewer still influence.

The soldiers of the First World War were, in theory, protected by international legislation. Agreed in 1898 and updated in 1907, the Hague Rules were the first truly international attempt to write into the statute books the rules of war as they applied to prisoners. Minimum rights to life and basic standards of treatment were expected of signatory nations, many of whom – Great Britain, Russia, France, Belgium and Germany – were to find themselves embroiled in war seven years later.

Yet men in smoke-filled meeting rooms were poor arbiters of what occurred between men on smoke-filled battlefields. At the moment of capture, many prisoners of war later admitted they thought it likely they would die. In a war where home-spun propaganda had taught men to hate the enemy for reported atrocities to soldiers and civilians alike, it took a great deal of trust for an unwounded man to hand over his weapon. Placing such reliance on the good nature of a captor, to whom no good had ever been ascribed, was difficult under any circumstances; in pitched battle such a gesture was an act of faith tantamount to leaving survival in the lap of the gods.

Enemy soldiers, pent up and aggressive, often gave prisoners short shrift during intense action. It was easier to kill than remove potentially dangerous prisoners from the battlefield, no matter how compliant they might seem when their hands were in the air. Many prisoners tried to forestall imminent death, holding up pictures of loved ones or mouthing words such as "Kamerad". Others, such as snipers, bombers or machine gunners, had been careful to remove badges that denoted their occupation before battle. These men could mete out death ruthlessly and so in turn often received short shrift from the enemy. But these attempts to appease or placate captors were little more than gestures. Survival depended on the enemy's feelings at the time. Had they seen many friends fall in the attack? Were they bent on taking revenge for some earlier loss, perhaps of friends or even brothers? Did they even care what happened to the enemy in the heat of battle? Were they acting on unwritten orders not to take any prisoners? No amount of gesturing could stop a summary execution if the enemy was intent on its taking place. Many soldiers at the front knew this because they themselves understood these feelings or had even been under similar orders. Some had seen prisoners shot and, if they had not, enough rumours or tales abounded of summary shootings to leave no one in any doubt that they occurred.

Once a prisoner's surrender had been accepted, the chances of survival improved but, even then, soldiers who maintained a look of defiance in their eyes or who appeared furtive or even too nervous, could still find life cut short. Prisoners were unavoidably anxious; many had never seen enemy soldiers before large numbers stormed their front line positions. Fear and shame were almost overwhelming, and even hardened sergeants were known, on occasion, to burst into tears. Prisoners offered or handed over belongings in order to curry favour, for enemy soldiers commonly liked souvenirs such as daggers, cap badges, watches or wallets. However, nerves were often frayed and misunderstandings common. Prisoners often recalled how, when lined up to be counted, they had interpreted the act as no more than the precursor to being shot. Occasionally, someone attempted to bolt, a natural inclination, not for reasons of patriotism so as to fight another day, but from the instinct to get away.

For the rest, the realisation that they were no longer soldiers but prisoners hit many men hard. All of a sudden they were entering a world for which they were totally unprepared. No sergeant at Tidworth had ever explained what it was like to be taken prisoner. Surrendering was just the age-old act of holding up hands high in the air, and was probably as much instinctive as learnt; after that a prisoner was on his own. He would be guided by events. Most captives followed orders as closely as possible, throwing away offensive weapons and dropping any other equipment or webbing. But as they did so, their innermost thoughts were often in turmoil. Some men felt disgrace at having been caught, others felt a great pain of loss, knowing as they did that they might not see their family again for years. Some were angry at being let down by neighbouring troops, many were simply relieved at knowing that their lives had been spared and that, for them, the war was over.

THOMAS SPRIGGS, born 2nd July 1897, died 31st January 2001, 55th Division Machine Gun Corps.

Of the thousands of British soldiers captured during the Battle of Cambrai in November 1917, Thomas Spriggs was the last survivor. Phlegmatic, pragmatic, unflappable, Thomas did not worry too much about whether he would live through the war or not. Why? Because he simply did not expect to survive. Having fought in the mud of Passchendaele, Thomas believed in the adage that if a bullet had your name on it there was nothing you could do to avoid it. Being killed was a likelihood; being wounded a certainty, but what Thomas least expected was to be taken prisoner of war, and in one piece too.

We attacked on November 20th 1917 and we were on the right flank and beyond us was all empty space, no front line, no nothing. It seemed to us that we had made a real break-through, but then the Germans counter-attacked on November 30th.

We were near a village called Villers Guislain when the machine gun team was captured. The first thing I recall is that the Germans first sent a plane over to take some photographs. We tried to shoot the plane down but didn't manage it and it swept round to the right of us and got all our artillery first, then us. In the morning we could see the Germans coming over and for some reason or other the machine gun would not fire more than one shot at a time before seizing up. I was number two on the gun, assisting number one, Paddy Shean, who was firing, and I can remember he cleared the gun, one shot and it jammed, cleared it, another shot and it jammed, cleared it, another shot, jammed. I wonder why it happened that particular morning? I could see the Germans gradually coming up and surrounding us, getting round the back.

Eventually, several soldiers came up above the slit trench we were in, led by an officer who waved a bomb at us and said, 'Drop your equipment and surrender' which we did. I distinctly remember when this man stood on the top of the trench with a handgrenade in his hand threatening to throw it at us, thinking, 'No, I'll be damned if I am going to hold my hands up to you'. It was undignified. Surrender to a bloody German, no fear. I wasn't going to put my hands up to them and say, 'Oh spare me, spare me, spare me'. I thought, if I am going to face a bullet or a bomb, then I will.

I'd been all through the third battle of Ypres, Passchen-daele and now Cambrai and I thought, 'Well, I'm going to get killed sometime, so why bother?' Pig-headed, I suppose. Of course being taken prisoner, that's something that never occurs to you when you're fighting, in fact I always thought I might be killed, which really didn't bother me a great lot; I thought, 'I'm going to get killed sometime, so why worry?' An officer must have been with us, because I remember that he understood a bit of German and told us to throw our equipment off. We climbed out and I remember thinking, 'I wonder what is going to happen now?'

ERNIE STEVENS, born 26th July 1899, died 29th November 1999, 20th Middlesex Regiment.

Despite losing his father to a sniper during the Boer War, Ernie Stevens never doubted that he wanted to be a soldier. Enlisting under age, Ernie was held back from active service until 1918 when, shortly before his nineteenth birthday, he was finally sent to France. Eager for front line experience, he entered the trenches on the 8th April; by the 9th he was a prisoner of war. I discovered Ernie quite by chance. A newspaper article reporting the Armistice Commemorations in Belgium in November 1998 paid tribute to a dozen veterans from Canada who had made the pilgrimage back to the Western Front. One veteran was quoted, Ernie, a lad from London, who'd emigrated to Toronto after the Great War.

There wasn't really a trench at all, all we had was a built-up earthwork that was quite a long way back from the front line. It was my very first night up the line since arriving in France but I didn't feel nervous. That's one thing I can't understand. Why was I so brave or ignorant? Ignorant, I think that is the right word, because I didn't know what was going to happen.

The night before I was captured had been very hectic and we were shelled, not with high explosive but with poison gas. I was tired and managed to sleep but the bombardment obviously woke me up many times. Everybody was alive to the fact that the Germans were strafing just behind our line where the reserves would be congregated, to try and knock them out as much as possible so as to leave just a few men in the first and second lines.

At daybreak, we learned that a ration party had come up with some bread and cheese and this was duly dished out. I had just got my share when suddenly the platoon sergeant shouted out, 'Stand To!' It was a very misty morning and we were in low-lying ground, but it was also quiet at this time and I don't recall any shelling. Two figures were seen coming through the mist and the platoon sergeant ordered us to fire five shots, rapid fire, thinking they were Germans. As soon as we started firing, up went their hands and as they approached we could see they had no helmets and that they had discarded their arms and equipment. They were our lads and luckily we had managed to miss them, perhaps through our own nervousness, but it was a very bad morning and it was difficult to see. One of them had a bullet wound in the back of his neck. The Germans had obviously reached our front line and had probably been reorganising for the next attack, and these two had managed to get away.

We stood behind the earthen wall we had built up when suddenly we heard this chatter of a machine gun behind us. We knew we were in for some trouble but we thought we were going to be attacked from the front, never imagining that we would be machine gunned from our rear. That was extraordinary. How did they get there? I mean, that's the first thing you think of. I heard the bullets whizzing past me as I made a run for a small slit trench and I jumped in to find myself up to my waist in water next to my platoon commander. He was new out to France and looked very worried. He turned to me and said, 'Corporal, I'm afraid we're absolutely hemmed in, it's impossible to make a fight of it. The only thing I can suggest is if you have a handkerchief bring it out, tie it to the end of your bayonet and indicate to the Germans that we are prepared to surrender.' I didn't want to do it but as an NCO I had to obey commands. I didn't like the idea of being in the hands of the Germans but we couldn't do a thing, and it's no good pretending to even try and fight against a machine gun and I don't know how many men.

I can assure you that that feeling of being taken prisoner was one of the worst you could ever have in your life. It was the most horrible thing I'd ever imagined could happen to me. It made me feel as if I was a coward. I was letting my country down, I was letting my unit down, I was letting my family down. A horrible, horrible feeling. I felt utterly bewildered; nothing ever occurred to me that could give me that kind of feeling, before or since, nothing. I was nearly sick thinking about it. Being taken prisoner, oh what a disgrace!

NORMAN COWAN, born 5th October 1898, died 26th February 2002, A Squadron Northumberland Hussars.

Norman Cowan was probably unique. He was almost certainly the very last surviving soldier in British military history to have ridden a horse into action. Surrounded by cavalrymen with drawn swords, Norman charged towards entrenched German positions on the Somme, only to be cut down by withering enemy fire. The date was 22nd August 1918, four years to the very day since British cavalry had launched the first attack of the British Expeditionary Force during the 1914-1918 war. Coincidences of date were not uppermost in Norman's mind, however, as he fought to stem the flow of blood from a serious leg wound. He was finally captured later that day.

The 22nd of August was a beautiful morning and we assembled in a railway cutting, ready to move forward. In the attack we were to be supported by Whippet tanks which were to go on and crush thirty-foot-deep barbed wire which our observation balloons had spotted in front of the German lines. Unfortunately, an officer of our regiment who was to lead the tanks was severely wounded and unable to carry forward the three tanks assigned to us. There was another problem too. Early that morning there had been an artillery bombardment during which the Germans had evacuated the front line and gone back into support. Then, as soon as the bombardment finished, they had moved back once more into their forward trenches.

Our 'A' Squadron was to lead the advance and at 6am we rode into action, the men with their swords drawn, pointing straight ahead, and myself, as corporal in charge of a Hotchkiss gun team, carrying a revolver. In retaliation, the German artillery quickly opened up on us from three directions. We pushed on into a field but found the deep belt of barbed wire untouched and, with trenches too, we were soon brought almost to a standstill. Through the mist and smoke, I saw our commanding officer, Colonel Rea, lying badly wounded and his orderly trying to carry him. I saw another soldier, Private John Charrington, fighting with the machine gun until he was badly wounded as well, then I saw my own officer, Lieutenant Patterson, a man from Hexham, shot off his horse. I followed Artie Lawson, my gunner, only to see his horse stumble and collapse, Lawson being thrown over her head to the ground. Then, moments later, I felt a sudden heavy thud in my thigh and was knocked off my horse and on to the ground. Straightaway I felt blood running down my leg, and I immediately thought that this was my blighty wound that would get me back to England. I threw my helmet aside but kept hold of my gas mask and crawled back on my knees, thinking 'blighty, home'.

I was getting weaker all the time and was almost unconscious when I reached the sunken road and fell in, virtually landing on Artie who had a bad flesh wound in his right shoulder. He looked at me and said, 'Norman, you are badly wounded. You are pouring with blood. Have you got a field dressing?' I told him 'Yes'. I opened my jacket and he ripped open the dressing kept in a little pouch inside. He took his jack-knife out and tore open my riding breeches right down to the knee and wrapped the dressing around my leg. Blood was still pouring through, so Artie said, 'I'm going to use mine on you'. There was another man there of the South Irish Horse, who had been seconded to our regiment, and he also gave me his bandage. I said, 'You are unwounded, go back, get out.' At first he refused to leave us but I said, 'I am ordering you to go back.' I was sinking into semi-unconsciousness but as he stood up to leave I seemed to see him with his head red and covered in blood. He left and Artie Lawson and myself lay there with firing going on all around and me with these three bandages soaking with blood. At about 5pm I woke to an acute pain in my upper leg. I was very thirsty and asked Artie for a drink, but both of us had discarded all our equipment except our gas masks. A while later Artie shook me and said, 'Germans on the bank' and looking I could dimly see three German soldiers with their rifles slung and all they said was, 'Come, Tommy, come!'

GEORGE GADSBY, born 4th March 1898, died 8th April 2000, 1/18th London Regiment (Irish Rifles).

Sadly, George Gadsby was the only veteran who was not interviewed to any great extent for this book. Aged 102, his memories of the war had faded over the years and he was no longer able to recall his time in action accurately. However, shortly after his return from the battlefields George wrote his memoirs, and extended extracts of his life as a prisoner of war are included. Fascinating in themselves, they also provide an interesting comparison between stories told soon after action and vivid memories recalled by other veterans over eighty years later.

16

Amid glorious sunshine we paraded one Sunday morning to be inspected by the Brigadier General and to pay honour to St Patrick. The General, in a brief address, voiced the history of the Division and expressed his appreciation of our fine turnout. I realised that still greater trials were before us (as such speeches were generally followed by some exciting event) and I could not but feel proud at belonging to such a well-disciplined Corps. We spent the next day in preparation for the Front and on the morning of the 20th we packed our limbers ready to proceed to take over the line at Welsh Ridge. After an unusually quiet tramp we arrived and took up position. My company, having executed the last front-line duty at Flesquières, was placed in the support trenches.

A terrific bombardment broke our slumber at 4 o'clock the following morning. A pineapple odour pervaded the air and we immediately put on our gas masks. The offensive had begun. Shells of every calibre continued to fall until 10am and the poisonous gas that emanated from most explosions necessitated our wearing masks for six hours with scarcely a respite. We received a telephone message stating the enemy had penetrated our front line and that they had subsequently been repulsed but not without heavy losses to our 'A' and 'D' Companies. However, owing to the battalion on our flank losing a little ground and the overwhelming number of the enemy, we were obliged to withdraw a few hundred yards from the Salient.

At dusk the Germans again made a violent bombing raid on our new position, reaching our Company line, but we successfully drove the enemy back inflicting heavy casualties with insignificant loss to our ranks.

The enemy, having been punished so severely in his evening encounter, kept very quiet on our front during the 22nd. Nevertheless, owing to the Huns pushing on our right and left flanks, the Divisional Commander ordered a general retirement in order to straighten our line. Our Colonel placed a machine gun at each post with one or two riflemen to stay and give an occasional "rat-a-tat-tat" until the majority of the Brigade had been withdrawn. We eventually arrived at Metz late in the evening, having been extricated from our perilous position without loss or knowledge to the enemy. Hungry and utterly exhausted, we lay down in the open and snatched a few hours' sleep.

I awoke early in the morning feeling happy that we had retired for a rest from the firing line. However, I was mistaken. A messenger came up a little later and informed Headquarters that the enemy was rapidly advancing in our immediate front. We were formed up and advanced towards the ridge in front of us, extended to right and left in open order.

On the ridge we encountered heavy machine gun fire and we made for a trench to find that it was only partly excavated, being scarcely three foot deep with practically no parapet. We crawled along to the right of the trench and endeavoured to reach the division reported to be on our flank, but the enemy held the intervening trench and we found ourselves confronted with rifle and machine gun fire. It was a horrible scene: our battalion was mixed up with two companies of another London division and we were confined in such a small length of trench that it was practically impossible for the wounded to pass along. We were penned in on three sides by the enemy and our only escape was to run across the open ground to our rear, which was swept with machine gun and rifle fire. We were to retire one following the next every few yards but the first four men fell dead in succession within five yards of the trench. I was then about fifth from the front man but fortunately the Colonel halted us and got out of the trench, changing the direction and running at a right incline to a trench a hundred yards to our rear. He fell after running the first fifty yards, but he was too artful for the Germans and got up and ran the remaining distance having outwitted the enemy who, like ourselves, took him for dead. We then followed his course one after the other and after the fastest sprint of my life I managed to reach the trench unhurt.

I soon discovered that this trench, like the one we had just left, was not connected with any other and that the next trench lay a further 200 yards behind. This we reached and were told to stay there until 6pm when we should be relieved. We were still out of touch with other troops and as the enemy still continued to press on our flanks, the order was passed along 'every man for himself'. There appeared to be only one chance of escape and we all jumped out of the trench and ran towards Ypres. The German infantry were firing at us from behind; his machine guns, which had advanced a considerable distance along our flanks, continued an unceasing fire on our depleted ranks, while his aeroplanes were nose-diving and pouring volleys from their guns. What a race for life! I was helping a comrade along who had been hit in the arm, my right leg almost touching his left, when another bullet penetrated his thigh. I did not know what to do for a moment but I looked round and saw that the German infantry were quite near and bullets were still spluttering the dirt at our feet. I had no option but to leave him again and run hard towards our next line in front of Ypres (formerly our rest camp). Here, elements of the Rifle Brigade and Machine Gun Corps were organised to make a stand whilst we continued to retreat to Rocquiney. Later in the evening, the Brigade was collected together (we numbered 53 out of a Battalion of 900) and were given food which we were eagerly waiting for, having had nothing for two days. We thought we were then going back right away from the line but instead we formed a composite company and were again placed in an old trench and told to 'dig in'.

We worked hard during the early part of the evening to make our trench serviceable. About 20 men who had been left behind to undergo courses of special instruction were brought up to re-inforce us and so the Sergeant allowed us to take a little sleep whilst the fresh troops carried on renovating the trench.

At 5pm we were told to 'Stand-To', as it was understood the Germans were again advancing in colossal numbers towards our new line. They came in sight about 8am and our artillery, which we had missed for a long time, were firing effectively and with great vigour on the enemy's massing columns that were collecting and advancing in a snake-like formation. When the Huns began to get nearer our line, however, the artillery retired and we were left to harass the enemy with our rifle fire. We had a very good parapet and made it hot for his advancing troops whilst we were not in any great danger of being hit. But alas! Our ammunition ran short and we were ordered to keep 15 rounds each until the last. Thus we stood on the parapet with fixed bayonets watching his artillery in the distance come into action and his infantry creeping on towards us.

During the early part of the morning, only one officer, a Captain, appeared to be present as the Germans pressed forwards. A squadron of thirty German planes came above our trench, and soon after, his artillery concentrated their fire on our communication trenches. The Germans then charged and broke through on our right and the only possible chance of escape was to retire together with the other withdrawing troops, but the officer would not give the order as he did not appear to realise he was in command. Too late. After many minutes had elapsed, the Germans occupied the rear of our trench and we found ourselves entirely surrounded.

JACK ROGERS, born 21st March 1894, died 13th April 2000, 1/7th Sherwood Foresters.

Jack Rogers had a great sense of humour. And rightly so, for he was heavily involved in the entertainment of troops during the war while performing with his Divisional Concert Party called 'The Crumps'. He recalled with clarity the time he was captured during the German March offensive of 1918 and continued to wonder what the enemy would have thought of him had they discovered the contents of his kit-bag: a blond concert party wig

and make-up. Born in Hammersmith, West London, Jack lived
for much of his life in Lincoln where he died aged 106.

We were in trenches near Bullecourt and prior to March 21st
we had been making raids on the enemy trenches at night,
capturing German prisoners, trying to find out what regiments were holding the line opposite and what the Germans'
plans for the near future were. The information showed that
the enemy was gathering its forces everywhere for a mighty
attack on a wide front which was due any time. Headquarters
were aware that I had not been home for some time, so I was
given leave to travel the day before my 24th birthday, so I
could be home on the day, 21st March 1918. Well, through
intelligence this date was found to be the launch of the great
German offensive. I'd written to my mother telling her not to
send a cake or anything like that because I was on my way
home, when, on the 19th, the army cancelled all leave.

Out in front of our line, working parties had been sent with
engineers in charge to dig a small extra trench, a slit trench,
cutting through our own barbed wire to get there. This was
being prepared for the expected attack and would be occupied solely by a few snipers, eight I believe, including me and
my two pals Charlie Shaw and Frank Richards. On the night
of 20th March, a group of us were sent in there. We took all
our equipment, everything we'd got, and we were told to
hold out as long as possible. We waited all night to see what
was going to happen, until at five in the morning the Germans
opened up with a big barrage.

We had anticipated they were going to make an attack
right across our front but nothing of the sort. The Germans
did not bombard the whole front, they left sections, shelling
to the left and right of us, very heavily too, but not directly on
us. The next thing we knew, German troops with all their
equipment were pouring through but we were still there,
holding onto our little trench, hanging on, just trying to have
a pot here and there. Eventually we looked around to the

back, where the ground went slowly down, and we could see Germans galore in every direction.

At about 11 o'clock, mopping up parties were sent out to clear little pockets of resistance, working their way round to us. They got nearer and nearer and they were sort of shouting – we weren't shooting. Then they began to throw in some of these potato mashers, as we called them, handgrenades. I saw one go over the top of us to the far end of our trench and I heard a bang. One chap was badly wounded in the legs and Frank got hit between the neck and the shoulder by a splinter of tin. He was holding his head down and it was bleeding. I looked at my mate Charlie Shaw and said, 'What do we do?' He says, 'It's no good, Jack, throw your hands up.' We realised it was hopeless, so we all just threw our guns at either end of the trench. There was nothing else to do, we just looked around and saw these blinkin' Prussian Guards come tearing down the trench.

I didn't know what to think. I could just see Charlie putting his hands up when I saw one guard coming straight for me, fixed bayonet, shouting in German. He came rushing up and from that moment I said goodbye – there was to be no more of me. I know the thought raced through my mind, 'What will be the feeling of this, a bayonet in my stomach? Will I know anybody or anything?' I expected the bayonet to go directly into me but it didn't. Strangely enough, when he got right up to me, and I swear the point of his bayonet was nearly touching me, he stopped, stood his gun down, looked at me and said, 'Zigaretten, Kamerad?' I nearly dropped to the ground in surprise. Whether he suddenly thought poor old devils, you know what I mean, I don't know, but I thought, my God, I'm still here and he wants a cigarette! Of all the things that anybody could ask for. I wondered if I'd heard him correctly but I felt in my jacket pocket where I carried a little tin of cigarettes I used to roll each morning and said 'Yes' and he took some and put them in his pocket, then pointed to my equipment and said 'Los'.

PERCY WILLIAMS, born 15th September 1899, died 28th May 2000, 1/5th Northumberland Fusiliers.

So powerful were the sustained attacks made on the British lines during March, April and May 1918, that many new recruits were thrust into the fighting with only the minimum of training. Percy Williams was one eighteen-year-old, among many, who found the horror of the Western Front almost too much to bear. The recollection of his capture was etched forever on his memory. Until his death, Percy lived in a retirement home on the Isle of Wight.

We were sent into a quiet sector that we had taken over from the French near Reims, a place called Fismes. We were just manning the lines, we didn't do anything, we thought we were just there to get acclimatised because the French had told us that nothing had happened in the sector for a couple of years. There was a bit of shellfire and a man called Sutton, a chap from Wakefield, was killed. He was the first of our young boys to die, then next a lad from Accrington was killed. But Sutton was a friend of mine, I'd met him in Doncaster when we were in the KOYLIs, then we were transferred to the Northumberland Fusiliers together. We were in C Company, and he was in my platoon; when a shell fell only fifty yards away and they told me, 'Poor old Sutton's had it', I was very upset and depressed.

It was pretty quiet until the 27th of May. I was in a dugout in the third line trenches when an officer came round and said that there might be action tonight. I'd not been under bad shellfire before and I was shaking and was almost sick with fright as we waited, just waited until all hell broke loose. When the guns opened up, the noise was deafening, the shells were falling, causing tremendous explosions and destroying not only the trenches above our heads but the stairs leading down to us. We were told to leave the dugout and we scrambled up into a trench that had been practically destroyed. Gas shells had been falling all night and saturated everything, covering our masks with a sulphur film. You couldn't see. I had stomach ache. I felt faint and sick and had to spew up, forcing me to take the gas mask off and vomit as best I could, trying not to breath in. A man next to me, I don't know who he was, he said, 'You must put on your gas mask, you must.' There was no chance, there were no officers that I saw and no communication at all because the bombardment was so terrific that the telephone lines were all smashed to pieces. I was absolutely terrified for hours, and the crying of the wounded – I'd never experienced anything so terrible in my life, and after only a month in France!

In the din we could hear casualties shouting for stretcher bearers, stretcher bearers, stretchers bearers. I thought, 'Oh my God, I'm going to die, I'm going to die!' We did not know what was happening, not fifty yards on either side of us. Then Corporal Collins came along. He was panicking, he'd seen tanks, he said that the Germans had broken through, and we were surrounded. 'Every man for himself, everything has collapsed,' he said, 'there's no chance, we must get out of it, otherwise we shall get captured.' As I stumbled from the trench I dropped my rifle, it was panic, the noise was terrible. I was weighed down by my pack, by fifty rounds of ammunition strapped around me, by my entrenching tool, the earth was blown up all around and I couldn't see. Then a shell burst close by, shrapnel wounding me in the leg. It wasn't bad, we had puttees on, but I saw my leg was bleeding and I remember having a towel to staunch it. I couldn't walk, so another chap said we'd better crawl for it, to try and get away.

By this time the gas had lifted and I could see the Germans running across, scores of them, I was so confused, you see, and the noise had left me all of a muddle, I didn't know where I was. Then I turned and saw this German with his fixed bayonet standing over me. He shouted 'Halt, halt, halt!' and then he motioned, 'or else', and grabbed me. I was petrified, I put my hands up. We were told in the newspapers a few months before that the Germans weren't taking any more prisoners, so you can imagine what I thought. He got hold of me, and ripped my spare ammunition off.

There was absolute panic. We could see the Germans in their grey uniforms, with their rifles and fixed bayonets; I had never seen a German before. I never saw a British officer, there was no command of any sort, we had to act on our own. A lot of the boys ran away to get out of it. You must remember that we were nearly all boys of eighteen and we were up against seasoned veterans, and when you see a lot of Germans coming with rifles and bayonets, well, I think you'd be a very brave man to wait until you were bayoneted, and they were big chaps, they looked so formidable in those big grey helmets. We were lads of eighteen, just boys.

FRANK DEANE, born 18th February 1899, died 28th October 2002, 1/6th Durham Light Infantry.

Frank Deane was standing in a trench just a few hundred yards away from Percy Williams on the day of their capture, 27th May 1918. Under the ferocious German onslaught, the front and second line trenches caved in, Frank being slightly wounded before being taken prisoner. In old age, Frank lived in a retirement home in the Lake District.

We were part of the 50th Division sent down to the French sector to gather ourselves together and to relieve some French regiments in the Reims area. The Northumberland Fusiliers were alongside us, just to the right of us. We were in trenches close to a couple of villages. One was called Corbeny, where a couple of chimneys were still left standing, while right behind our lines was Chaudardes.

We were in or near the front line in little pockets of three or four people, far enough apart that we never saw our neighbours, which shows how spread out we must have been. I think they felt they couldn't do anything with us, I think they just thought we were expendable. We'd been up the line three or four times by then.

The Germans launched a fierce bombardment and we just sat in the trench while all this stuff just crashed all around us. Everything you can think of was coming over, shrapnel and heavy shells and gas shells. We had been told that our artillery would bombard their trenches at 9pm, the night before. Well, there was a bit of artillery fire from our side but they started at midnight and there wasn't a whisper from ours after that. All we could do was to sit quietly on the firestep in the dark and listen, just hoping nothing dreadful would hit us.

As it was dark, you got the flashes of light from the shells and the Very lights. It wasn't just the bangs and shrieks of shells but, you see, whenever a shell fell, earth would come down and it would rattle on your tin hat because it would spread for quite a long way from the point of impact. You just shrug your shoulders and get as much of yourself under your tin hat as you possibly can and hope for the best. After all if you walk from one place to another, you wouldn't be any better off so there was nothing to do except sit down, be terrified, and wait until it was all over. It's nothing you can describe. You were just stunned and shrinking a little bit, shivering when you thought something was hitting a bit too near. Suppose somebody was standing over you with an axe and they were going to chop off your head – what would you feel like? – could you describe your feelings to anybody? – I don't think so.

A shell was heard that didn't explode but made a fizzing noise, somebody shouted 'Gas!' I put my mask on and was all right. However, I later looked at my silver watch and the gas had blackened the edges of the metal. At about 7am there was a thick mist and the Germans came across. When it got a bit lighter we looked up over the top and we saw a mass of Germans, I suppose about 100 in a square. They were well to the right and to the rear of us, marching quite quickly. When we saw these men, there was nothing for us to do but to scuttle further back into our trenches to see if we could get ahead of them, because if we just sat where we were we'd have been surrounded there and then. We seemed to be on our own, but presently a few others joined us and we made our way back. There was only a lance corporal who was in charge of our little group but somehow or other we managed to keep together all the way. He was an old soldier, a nice old chap and his name was Lindsey, a coal miner in civilian life. I can't remember a lot, everything was confused, but I recall seeing my platoon officer and he was just sat on the firestep with two men doing absolutely nothing, he just watched us go by and didn't say a word. He seemed to me to be just waiting there until the Germans caught up with him. I don't know if he actually knew what was going on or whether he was just dumbfounded. That was the only other party of our battalion that I saw that day, so you can imagine that we must have been terribly scattered in little tiny groups. We left the trenches and passed through a wood, crossing a road, the Chemin des Dames they called it, then up a sloping hill on the other side. A couple of officers on horseback were on that hill, where they'd come from I don't know, possibly headquarters, and it was they who lined us up on the hill facing these woods waiting for the enemy.

The Germans came through, firing their machine guns like billy-ho. We'd been lying low for protection when to the right of us a trench was spotted and we were told to get up and go to this trench. I was next to the last man, a lance corporal, but we never got anywhere near the trench before they were all around us and I was captured. I can't remember a lot, it was all very confused. I do know that just before I was captured, I was wounded. A machine gun bullet crashed through the first joint of my thumb before going up my hand. My corporal friend next to me said, 'Your hand is bleeding.' I didn't know I'd been hit. He took my first aid patch off my jacket and he put it on and I would guess it stayed there for a week and was never looked at.

When I was captured I don't think I had any feelings of any kind as far as I remember. I daresay I was a bit jittery. The funny thing about being in the army, you get so used to doing as you are told you just don't think about anything. It was funny how you took everything for granted when you were in the army. You went where you were sent, and you did as you were told, and you had no thought for tomorrow.

TOMMY GAY, born 25th April 1898, died 19th February 1999, 2nd Royal Scots Fusiliers.

He considered himself 'the luckiest man alive', and Peckham-born Tommy Gay believed it too. Having survived the disastrous British offensive on 1st July 1916, Tommy went over the top on at least one further occasion before his capture at Guillemont, a devastated village on the Somme. With his battalion annihilated and sniper fire everywhere, Tommy sheltered in a shell hole, only to find a German pressing a bayonet against his chest. With life expectancy seriously in the doldrums, Tommy fought a new battle to survive, spending much of the next two and a half years down a German coal mine. He lived to tell the tale, returning to England where he comfortably reached his 100th birthday.

They had been bombarding Guillemont for days non-stop and the place was blown to pieces. We were to launch what was a third attack on the village and we were given a dose of rum before the off. Oh yeah, you feel you could go and fight anything after a good old dose of rum, it bucks you up entirely. We went over the top and when we went in, there was fire from all directions, bullets pinged past, you could hear how close they were. There were machine guns and snipers all over the place. We lost no end of men, shocking. I remember as we climbed the barbed wire my clothes became all ripped up, like rags. It was a bit of a struggle to get out, getting caught on the wire. Oh, I was in a hell of a state. Some of the chaps were lying around, you know, arms off, in pain, but you couldn't help the poor souls, you couldn't help them at all. We were just finished, in a shell hole, trying to hide out of the way so that we could escape back to our lines. I was in no man's land in a shell hole when I was captured, along with three or four others, men of another regiment I think. We'd run out of ammunition, no Mills bombs or anything, so all we could do was bury ourselves in a shell hole until it got dark, when we would have been able to creep back home to our lines. All of a sudden a German appeared unexpectedly, bawling out in German. When I saw him come up to me I was really shocked, I couldn't understand it, couldn't make out where he'd come from, actually. It seems we had got right above some sort of command post, because this German came up some stairs close to where we had taken refuge. He was bawling and of course we didn't know what he was talking about, waving his gun with a fixed bayonet. He had a good mind to stab me and finish me off, I remember turning cold, the coldest feeling I ever had, he pressed his bayonet against my chest, jabbering away as if to say, 'I've got a good mind to stick this through you,' but he hesitated. The lads with me, I thought they were going to set about him, so he left me alone. He told us, 'Los, los', 'come on get up', and we had to follow him, which we did and he marched us back behind his lines to a compound where several of our men were already waiting. We weren't allowed to talk, they were watching us you know, they had a guard on us all the time, so we just milled around on our own, until we were ordered away. I don't think I felt anything at all at the time, I'd done my share, I'd done what I could, that was all. I had done my duty and I was now a prisoner and where I was going, I didn't know any more than a fly.

FREDERICK HAMMOND, born 27th September 1897, died 18th April 1999, 1/8th Lancashire Fusiliers.

Not many soldiers ever survived the injuries that Frederick Hammond received during an attack on the 25th March 1918. Cut down by a bullet through his head and punctured by shrapnel, Frederick lay in the open all day, dropping in and out of conciousness. Picked up by the Germans, he was to spend the next seven months mostly in a German hospital before being sent to Switzerland for the remainder of the war. He was as pleasantly surprised as anybody that he managed to live to be 101 years old. A quiet but very personable man, Frederick lived independently near Hemel Hempstead.

There was a sharp frost in the morning, very cold, and we were lined up on a wide open space. There was a slope which ran upwards to the top of a ridge where the Germans were entrenched. I don't remember any instructions nor any preliminary barrage before we went in, so that when we advanced they were just mowing us down, it was dreadful to see, men falling around me, killed. I had gone only a little distance when I got a bullet through the jaw and I fell. The bullet went in behind my ear and came out the other side in the middle of the cheek. I was knocked to the ground, my mouth full of blood. I was near a sunken road and I rolled down the bank where I was hit by some shrapnel, might have been from one of our shells, I don't know, but I was unconscious for some time and then I saw my mother. My mother was there, I saw her standing there, I don't know why, but I have never mentioned that to anybody until last year. I came round when it was still light and I thought that our troops might counter attack, but when it was getting dark a lone German came along, walking up and down the road. I pretended I was dead and he passed me a few times but it was getting dusk, so I thought I would have to give myself up. I was wounded in the leg, hand and back. I was lying there most of the day

He was kind to me and made me a sort of crutch to go along and took me back to the Red Cross post where I got better treatment than I ever got in the camps. It was the only time I was given a proper dressing on my wound. They wanted us to move on, three or four of us, to another place during the night but we refused to go. It was March and I was lying in a bed and the fellow next to me was dead so I took his coat off to keep myself warm.

WALTER HUMPHRYS, born 5th September 1897, died 17th April 2003, 1/15th London Regiment (Civil Service Rifles).

To have survived 18 months on the Western Front is no mean feat in terms of the First World War, and Walter Humphrys remembered them all. With great clarity, he recalled the near misses and the moments of luck he had from the time he arrived in France in December 1916 until his capture in March 1918. His luck ran out on the 23rd of that month when his unit, part of the Third Army, became surrounded by the enemy and he was taken prisoner. Rather than being sent to a camp in Germany, Walter was kept in France for eight gruelling months, working close to the battle lines with little to eat. Afterwards, he felt reticent about recalling his experiences. Born and raised in the Mendip Hills, he lived in a residential home in Ealing until his death, aged 105.

On the morning of the attack, a few Highland Light Infantry came round the corner of the trench and told us the Germans were going through the lines in droves. This was news to us. We didn't know what was going on. We were in the front line and had all the shelling and the gas attacks, but we seemed to avoid where the Fifth Army, the neighbouring army to us, had given way. It all meant that by the evening we were right up in the air, as all during the day the Germans had streamed through behind us.

As the number one in a Lewis gun team, I was told to remain behind to give the Company a chance to retire to a makeshift trench. After an hour or so, we picked the Lewis gun up and went into a valley behind, into the trench, and joined the rest of the company. We were told that the Germans had swept by us on our flank but that there was a company of our people put on a ridge just behind us to protect our rear. But in the morning when dawn came, instead of a company to protect us, the Germans were firing down on us. Somebody gave the order to charge these Germans behind us as soon as the light was sufficient. I don't know who gave the order but it was a toss up as to whether it was a wise thing to do or not. We went over the top to try and break through without any covering fire and we were wiped out by about halfway. I was right on the flank because I had been the last person to go in the trench the night before, so I stood out a little bit to the side of the bulk of men and I found that everybody had gone down. I dropped down quickly on to my back with my heels towards the Germans up there and pushed my way back down the slope, turning a somersault into the trench. When I got in there, there was another man, a big fellow, I don't know whether he had gone over the top or not. I was crouched behind him, in this shallow trench, looking over his shoulder when I heard a ping and I saw the bullet come out from behind his ear. The bullet had gone through his tin hat and he didn't move. He couldn't have been conscious of it at all, absolutely gone in a split second. I waited nearly all day wondering what was going to happen. Later in the afternoon I heard a lot of shouting from the German side and I popped my head up quickly and saw three lines of Germans coming down on the trench, so I scrabbled up the other end to see if there was anybody up that end. I found about half a dozen men, that was all. We couldn't get up because we would have been shot from behind, so we waited until they were right on top of us and then we gave ourselves up. I'd been captured about 4.30pm on 23rd of March 1918.

They were quite reasonable and didn't rough us up at all but just passed us down to the people behind. We just got up and put our hands up. In international law, if you give yourself up they are supposed to accept your surrender, but if you resist they can shoot, as happened once when I was in a battle at Bourlon Wood, terrible place, where I had taken two German prisoners. The Germans had attacked as we were about to retire, and had got in behind us. I was on my own because of casualties and I came across two German machine gunners and they put their hands up. I only had a rifle, as I was no. 4 in the team then. I pointed to our destination and we started off. Soon after, an officer came up and said, 'I'll take charge of these' and he took them and went off at a tangent for the same trench I was making for. After a little while I looked over to see how he was getting on and they'd stopped and evidently one of the Germans was refusing to go or something like that. One was talking to the other in an offensive sort of way, but I don't know what they were doing, because the officer shot him and went on with the other man. He was justified, because if the prisoner resists you can shoot him. If you are a prisoner you have to do what you are told, otherwise you can become a danger.

WILLIAM EASTON, born 15th October 1898, died 18th August 1999, 77th Field Ambulance, RAMC.

The pictures of Bill Easton seem to show a boy aged eighteen going on fifteen. It is hard to imagine him struggling across the mud-soaked battlefield around Ypres, dealing with atrocious wounds and carrying the wounded to safety. He enlisted at sixteen but was only called up two years later in March 1917. He served for around ten months at the front before he was captured, his apparent youth affording him protection given both by other prisoners and, on occasion, by his captors. His captivity is one of the more extraordinary stories of life as a POW, a story Bill told with almost photographic precision. He lived at home in Kings Lynn, where he had been most of his life. Fit and well to the last, he died peacefully in his sleep.

One night in late November 1917, my unit was withdrawn from the Ypres Front. There were not many of us left, and we no longer had enough men to make up an ambulance unit, so we were told to wait for reinforcements. I was on supply, which meant I could be sent anywhere to fill a gap, so eventually I was sent by truck to join another unit. I had no idea what was going on, but I was supposed to meet an officer of the Norfolk Regiment. I arrived in the line on the 20th of March 1918, and I met a sergeant who knew nothing about this officer I was supposed to meet. He was new out to the Front and was with about forty conscripts, all of whom had been in the army only about three months.

They were in this trench, standing-to as if they were expecting an attack, and were frightened out of their lives. All afternoon they stood there and I said to this sergeant that it was unusual to have them standing to all that time, and was there a chance of a cup of char? He swore at me and was most offensive: 'What do you think this is, a bloody restaurant?' he asked me. After dusk he did let the men rest. It was cold that night and I simply stopped in that trench and listened to these boys moaning. Well, early in the morning the Germans came over, they were kicking up a hell of a row, it was pitch black at first, then as it got lighter we could see them in their thousands, as far as you could see across the fields, singing and shouting. This sergeant hadn't got a clue what was happening and eventually turned to me and asked, 'Shall we fire on them?' but I said 'No'. We could see these Germans, the nearest were about 150 yards away, but they never came towards us. At about the same time, on our left, I saw a whole block of our lads leave the trenches, running like the devil. I said, 'The Germans are bypassing you. They'll go so far and then stop and when they're ready, they'll come back and pick us up.' 'Do you think so?' he said. 'I jolly well know so,' I replied.

After they'd passed us by, I told the sergeant that I was going over to the trenches that our boys had evacuated. 'What the devil are you going there for? There's nobody there?' I told him I knew that, but we didn't have any rations that I could see and as our lads had left in such a hurry, there was bound to be food there. I asked if I could take someone with me but the sergeant refused, so I set off and went into one or two dugouts and found a tin or two of bully beef and some biscuits, rather like dog biscuits. After I returned, one man, who'd gone to try and get back to our troops, came back into our trench after wandering around for a while. He'd still got his weapon, and I said to him, 'It's hopeless, we're surrounded, and there are hundreds of the brutes nearby, so you'd better get rid of the rifle.' I noticed that several of these young chaps had kept their blinkin' guns and I said to the sergeant, 'You'd better tell them to dump them.' The sergeant said, 'Oh, they've only just got them.' 'Well, if they have them much longer there'll be a few rifles without men,' I replied.

I don't know who the lad was who'd kept his rifle, but he didn't seem to understand that we were already prisoners. The Germans were using loudspeakers, calling on pockets of resistance to surrender. However, he'd still got his rifle knocking about when the Germans surrounded us, and they promptly shot him. I thought it was such a pity, but it was his own fault, he ought to have known when to give his weapon up.

CHAPTER TWO

The Weary Road

The 21st March 1918 was by far the worst day for the British Army as regards prisoners of war. In the space of a few hours, some 21,000 British soldiers were captured, far more than on any other comparable day in the war, and by the end of the initial battle on 5th April a further 54,000 had been taken. Such were the numbers of POWs that many survivors were simply stripped of their weapons and webbing and shown the direction which they were expected to follow. They were then abandoned to join the crowds streaming across the German front and second lines, as the enemy pressed on with their overwhelming attacks. This day was exceptional. As a rule, prisoners were marched back from the line under the escort of one, perhaps two guards, the urgency of the situation at the front dictating how many men could be spared to take back or collect -prisoners. Those prisoners fit to walk often made temporary stretchers from ground sheets or duckboards to carry wounded comrades and enemy. As they walked back, weary and deflated, they would often pass enemy soldiers marching towards the line, when they were as likely to receive a cigarette as a clip round the head. Some would be sworn at, others stared at, many just ignored as they trudged across a field or, more often, down the road towards a holding pen where prisoners would be congregated before being sorted out and moved on.

These men were not necessarily safe. Friendly fire, as it is now known, caused innumerable deaths as British gunners sought out enemy transport or opposing gun batteries in the back areas. Prisoners frequently recall shells falling in fields to their left or right, men instinctively ducking. Similarly, machine gun bullets fired over long distances took toll. At least one prisoner I spoke to recalled a man dropping dead next to him while they were marching away. He had been shot in the back, by which side was unclear, but certainly not by anyone in the immediate vicinity.

The pens in which the prisoners were eventually congregated could be several miles behind the lines, and stops were made along the way, men collapsing to sleep where they fell, through exhaustion and nervous fatigue. Guards, free from control, could be brutal at times and there are depositions from former POWs claiming that prisoners incapable of keeping up were manhandled or even killed. Certainly, prisoners interviewed for this book told how the German Uhlans were frequently provocative and violent, lances and horses being used to jostle the prisoners as they walked.

Once they reached a pen or wire cage, few would stay more than a day or two, as no facilities were supplied other than perhaps a trench for a midden. Most slept on the ground to await further instructions, during which time irregular and usually very poor quality food was sent into the cage. Even though trench warfare ensured that the opposing sides were almost always in close proximity, surprisingly few soldiers saw the enemy up close, even in action. In such circumstances, the prisoners' cage frequently attracted German soldiers who wandered up to have a closer look at the enemy, dishevelled and hungry and not half as fearsome as they had been led to believe. Often bartering took place, in which soldiers who had managed to hold on to rings or watches traded all their worldly goods for a chunk of bread or a piece of sausage.

If they were not held in cages, men were often taken to old factories, even churches, to spend a night or two where, in an ideal world, they would be given cards to fill out which gave the basic details that Private X of Y Battalion had been captured. These would be forwarded to Britain via the Red

Cross, letting families know of their loved ones' capture. This information would be passed on to the military authorities who would post men as prisoners and later arrange for food parcels to be sent. Meanwhile, wounded men would be separated and taken to a first aid post or a clearing station for basic medical treatment.

Until 1918, most prisoners were sent to Germany to the hundreds of camps and work Kommandos situated right across the country. The trip entailed walking to the nearest major railhead where they would be placed in locked cattle trucks, perhaps as many as fifty at a time. Conditions were usually appalling, packed as they were like sardines, with no toilet, little food, and perhaps no rest stops between France and the interior of Germany. Early on in the war, some of the first prisoners were exhibited to the civilian population, trains pulling in to major junctions such as Cologne, where the doors were opened and the human cargo forced to endure insults and abuse. However, as prisoner of war trains became more frequent, most trains were allowed to pass uninterrupted, save for the odd stone thrown at the passing wagons.

ERNIE STEVENS

Attacked and then surrounded, Ernie had little option but to follow his officer's instructions and signal their willingness to surrender. Having been in France only a matter of days, Ernie felt humiliated.

There was no earthly chance of us getting away, the Germans were in such numbers, so I waved my dirty handkerchief and in due course a German appeared on the level ground above us, looking down and ordering us out of the trench one by one. The first thing we had to do was to throw off our equipment which lay strewn all over the place, and then I noticed Sam Simpkins, a mate of mine, lying on the ground moaning, obviously hurt very badly. I asked a German for permission to go and have a look at him and he nodded. I ran over and it was then that I saw that Sam had been hit in the left arm. His elbow had been shot away and his forearm was only hanging on to his upper arm by a piece of flesh no thicker than a finger. I knew nothing about first aid but Sam was in a very bad way, blood was pouring out and I knew he would be dead within ten minutes. I had to stop the bleeding somehow, so I asked permission to pick up a knife and the German nodded quite vigorously, like hurry up and do it. He seemed to give a little smile as much as to say, 'Good, I'm glad someone's going to do something' and very quietly and slowly, I hope without harming Sam, I cut his sleeve off almost to his shoulder. Sam was in a semi-conscious state as I made two strips out of the sleeve, which I used as tourniquets above his elbow. I stopped the bleeding but I couldn't do anything about his forearm, so it was just a case of gently getting his arm and laying it across his breast.

There were eight of us altogether in that trench. I knew just behind there was a duckboard, very mucky, very wet and very heavy. Our officer was taken away, I didn't see him again, so being an NCO I ordered these chaps to bring the duckboard over, three on one side, three on the other and gently lift Sam onto it. We waited around for some time before moving off, taking it in turns to carry the duckboard on our shoulders. I can assure you it was heavy going. We went from our second line up to the first line, over no man's land, over the German first and second lines, and -eventually onto a road and towards a German first aid tent where we put Sam down.

As we did this, a German medical officer came out. He looked at Sam, returned to the tent and immediately came back with a scalpel and he just cut Sam's forearm off and threw it on a heap of other arms and legs and what have you, some in German uniform, some in khaki, they were easy to distinguish. The heap was about knee high and wide, perhaps 50 in all, and, well, to be frank, the first thing you want to do is be sick. It's an awful sight to see such a pile of limbs. Unfortunately that is what you see in war.

Another ten or fifteen British soldiers had congregated at the First Aid tent and with them we were marched off and put into a wire cage for three days' during which time they gave us only half-a-dozen emergency rations like dog biscuits to eat, and nothing to drink. It's beyond my comprehension – and they had everything to be gloating about – but it was not a fair way of dealing with unfortunate prisoners who couldn't do anything about it, and that's what you are, you're a prisoner of war.

GEORGE GADSBY

Our captors treated us fairly well. One of them struck me across the back with a stick saying, 'Ah we la victorie'. I expected more, as we had inflicted heavy casualties, but I did not suffer anything else in going to the enemy's rear. When we reached Léchelle, we formed into small groups and were told to carry the wounded. They had no stretchers and we had to carry both the Germans and our own patients in a waterproof sheet tied to a pole. We deposited them at a hospital and then set out on the march.

We had not been going long when we realised what a terrible state Germany was in. The roads were blocked with transport, two and three motor cars were lashed together and pulled by the power of the front one, and vehicles (not much better than orange boxes on wheels) were packed so heavily that they creaked under the weight. Although we realised what privations confronted us, we could not but raise a smile as we marched along. The Germans' transport reminded us of a travelling circus. Behind each cart generally followed a cow, whilst on the top of the loads could be seen a box of rabbits or fowls. A motor car came dashing along the road, evidently containing German Staff Officers. They were wearing their high coloured hats and resembled proud peacocks rather than soldiers.

What a pandemonium! Now and then a troop of dusky cavalry mounted on bony ponies passed us on the way, whilst battalions of infantry led by martial music (which did not sound much better than the noise made by a youngster kicking a tin along the road) advanced to the front with stooping heads looking particularly fed up and worn out.

At last the traffic began to subside and we continued marching in a mechanical sort of way until we had covered about 19 miles, when we halted for the night and sought our abode in a barbed wire field. Hungry and thirsty, we were left to sleep as best we could.

At 3am they brought two buckets of water for 300 men and after a struggle I got a little drink. At 7am a patrol of old and evil-eyed Prussians mounted on horseback arrived to escort us to our destination. It was a terrible march across the old battlefields. One road we passed along was strewn with dead horses from the top to the bottom and as we were then a considerable way beyond our own original front line, it can be surmised that they had been left lying there since our advance on Cambrai last November. This was not, however, the worst sight we witnessed on this sickening journey. Two or three British soldiers lay at the roadside. One was partly covered by a blanket whilst the others appeared to have no covering. Their boots and socks had been removed. It was a ghastly disgrace to a country professing to be civilised; no excuse could be given for leaving them so long, as I think no shell had fallen anywhere near since last November.

JACK ROGERS

We had all just surrendered at the last minute, but you know we'd been holding out right up until half past eleven and this attack had started early in the morning. How did you know what to do? You didn't know what to do. You don't stop to think how am I going to become a prisoner of war, you just throw your hands up and hope this fellow won't do what it looks as though he's going to do.

What were my feelings? Absolute relief. With a German rushing towards me with a fixed bayonet – he'd got no reason to like me in any way – I thought this was the finish, it's the only thing you can think of. So to put his gun down and ask for a cigarette, I just couldn't believe it, extraordinary relief. The last thing in the world we thought of being was a prisoner of war. We had never anticipated such a thing. Of course then you start thinking of what is going to happen to you now, what's it going to be like to be a -prisoner of war. Unquestionably there's a fear for the future, you often heard about the way prisoners of war were treated or maltreated, being sent down coalmines and that sort of thing.

Any equipment had to be taken off and left with our kit bags and sandbags on the trench floor, while we climbed out on top of the parapet. Frank was feeling pretty shaky and couldn't walk very well, so he put his arms round our necks and we dragged him away up a slope. There was quite a lot of walking then, you could see prisoners in all directions going back. The three of us hadn't got very far when a young German officer came up to us – a very smart looking fellow, I can see him as plain as if it were now – and said in English better than I could speak, 'Where are you from?' pointing at me. I didn't know what to say, but said 'London'. 'Oh, London,' he said, 'So am I. I was at Birkbeck College but they brought me home, and now I'm in this lot. Anyway, you're lucky, the war's over for you, get on your way.' Off he went and off we went, to walk back as prisoners of war: my 24th birthday.

We were on our own and we walked about not knowing quite where to go. Dishevelled-looking prisoners were coming in from all directions and someone urged us towards a sunken road where there were broken vehicles and dead horses everywhere. We just followed everyone else until we finally reached a great big field and there we stopped all night, nothing to eat, nothing to drink. In the morning, the Germans brought this big dixie on a sort of trolley. They gave us a tin each of tea-like liquid from this dixie and one slice of brown bread. From then onwards we began to be ushered into groups. I lost all my pals, Charlie and Frank – I don't know what became of them – before we were taken here, there and everywhere, marching along behind anyone until we got to what appeared to be a goods station. Here we had to await a long line of cattle trucks, forty men to a truck. Some steps were brought for us to walk up into the truck and they packed us in as fast as they could, all blacked out, with just a little square ventilator, like grating, right up in the corner to give us air. We travelled in this truck for two days, still with no water or food, and the only place we could use as a toilet was one corner of the wagon chosen amongst ourselves for us all to use. The men had sense enough to go there, but there was no drainage, the urine just ran out at the bottom of the truck. The smell was awful and it was as much as I could do to hold a handkerchief against my nose for a while. You were standing up, you'd have to lean up against the wall of the truck. Those in the middle got no support at all except by leaning against one another until they'd slide down, and then they'd get up again and slide down once more. I didn't know anyone, and half the time I was pushing up against someone to keep my balance. It's practically dark most of the time, you can't see where you are or where you're going, you can only hear the reverberation of the music of the wheels on the lines as they're going along, rackety bang. Well, as a matter of fact I think you wouldn't be sorry if you died. If that isn't enough to drive anybody mad, I don't know what is.

PERCY WILLIAMS

I had to remove all my equipment and take off my gas mask and steel helmet. I can remember the lingering smell of gas in the air which affected my breathing, then, after about quarter of an hour, a couple of prisoners came along with a ground sheet and pole and carried me a little way before they got me on my feet. My leg was very painful and bleeding but I was able to hobble along back to the German lines. We were not out of danger, as one of our own shells burst only fifty yards away at one point. I could hear it whizzing and saw the explosion, but thankfully nobody was hit; it made me think that our own bombardment was nothing to deter the Germans. When we stopped, a German asked us if we were American or English, then he said, 'Don't worry, we are not going to kill you, but if you show any resist-ance or try and run away, you'll be shot.' And that put our minds at rest. I was taken to a little dressing station about half a mile behind their lines where they put a bandage on my leg. We were all dazed, sort of shellshocked, the drum in my ear had been affected and I had difficulty hearing anything. It took a while to collect myself. I felt awful because we had been running away, I felt like a coward but there was no alternative, we were just on our own. For a couple of days we slept out in the open. Then they took us to a village called Abbé Fontaine, not far from Laon, and put some barbed wire around us, and eventually an electric light was rigged up to see that we did not try and escape at night. A funny thing happened there. Within a couple of days of our capture the Germans came to see us and asked if there were any Irishmen amongst us, or anyone with Irish connections. A corporal said that he was Irish, and a couple of others spoke up as well and they were taken from us to another camp. We never saw them again. We were puzzled at the time, but later I learnt that the Germans segregated some Irishmen who were keen to stir up trouble in Ireland.

The weather was hot and the trenches that we dug to use as latrines had to be filled in after only a day or two because of the stink and the thousands of flies. We had no such thing as toilet paper either, not even newspaper, so we used dock leaves to clean our behinds. After a few weeks my leg was getting better, so I was put to work carrying water in billycans and digging more latrines. Each morning we simply had a bit of black bread and then a few potatoes with their jackets on – well, fair enough – only glad to have them, but we were always hungry and always filthy dirty. One day in seven we were given off, when we were able to take our shirts and pants off to kill the lice in our clothes, but we stayed in our khaki for months, and not until I was in a camp at Bremer-haven were we given clothes.

FRANK DEANE

The Germans cut the webbing of our equipment, they didn't bother to search us or interfere with us at all. Other prisoners told me later that they had been stripped of all their valuables, but I wasn't and I did have one valuable, a watch. My father gave it to me for my fifteenth birthday and I carried it with me in a little strap around my waist, through the war and ever since. We were then marched off back across our trenches and onwards, behind the German lines. That night we spent out in the open, then marched further back. I became quite cheerful because they seemed to have such a ramshackle lot of trans-port, an old harvest cart being pulled by a donkey, a mule and a horse. I didn't see any motor transport, so I thought, well, if that's the sort of equipment they've got, they won't last long; I felt quite optimistic.

I did stay out one night and it was a lovely summer's day, as I remember, so it was quite nice and warm as we slept. The next day we went in a train, in fourth class carriages as they called them in those days – just wooden benches – into

Germany. I think it took two or three days to get to Kassel. My bullet wound was a lucky shot as it happened, because it meant I went straight into hospital where I stayed for about two months as it took a long time to heal.

NORMAN COWAN

After the cavalry charge had failed, Norman had no option but to surrender to the Germans. With a serious wound in his leg, the need to seek medical treatment was now imperative.

I tried to stand up but my left leg gave way. One of the Germans scrambled down and, with Artie supporting me on one side and the German on the other, we moved back in the direction of a field dressing station where we were left lying on the ground. I was told that I was now a prisoner of war. At some point while I was there, two officers came along, one was a colonel of the artillery and the other a colonel in a machine gun unit. Apparently they were in some sort of dispute as to who had been doing the most damage when we attacked, and through an interpreter I was asked if I had received my wound from cross fire, but I passed out.

Soon after, four soldiers with a wooden door and an army blanket thrown over it came and lifted me up and took me to a casualty station. I was put onto a metal table and there I lay until I took my turn to be operated on. I was dead scared, terrified, and I became more terrified as I lay on this table while men were operated on around me. An officer came along, but with so much congealed blood he had difficulty examining me. However, in good English he told me that I had a nasty upper thigh wound and the bone had been chipped. 'Now look,' he said, 'are you frightened?' I said, 'I'm terrified.' He said, 'Well, don't worry, I've spent two years before the war at Guy's Hospital in London. I'm going to send you to sleep and when you wake up you'll find a bit of tissue paper, hold on to it.' He then put a mask over my face.

The next thing I knew was that I was lying in a bunk and very feverish. I opened the tissue paper and there was a bullet in my hand. There were a number of other wounded there, many in pain. Above me was a young German soldier, in great distress and he said, 'Tommy, Tommy, take this, take this.' I shook my head in refusal at first but from the top bunk he handed over a little purse. I managed to open it and found some French coins. He died the next morning from the effects of gas and wounds, two orderlies coming in to carry his body away.

The stretcher cases were now sent in primitive railway carriages to a warehouse that had been refitted as a large casualty hospital at a place called Le Cateau. It was a weary trip. British soldiers were coming in wounded all the time and I remember one Highlander, badly wounded, saying, 'It's all right lads, they're beaten, they're moving back.' I was given a bed with a pulley and weight arrangement to support my left leg. The roof of the hospital appeared to be mostly glass and at night, when the sky was clear, I was able to gaze through and see our fighter planes coming in over the hospital.

The ward was run by a sister of tremendous size who ruled it with a rod of iron but was greatly respected by everyone. One clear night when I lay awake in my bed, I heard a plaintive voice crying out, 'Will no one help me? I cannot see anything at all.' As I listened, the voice seemed familiar to me and came from the third row of beds immediately behind me. The request for help went on and on and was disturbing, so I decided to try and locate the chap. To do this, I had to disengage my leg from the pulley arrangement. This I did with much difficulty and in spite of protests from German soldiers on either side of me, warning that the big nurse would be very angry, I struggled up and by clutching the bed rails I managed to find this soldier. He turned out to be one of my Hussar companions sitting up in bed with his eyes heavily bandaged and all covered with corrugated paper bandages. He turned out to be Billy Watson from Gilsland, one of our own North-umberland Hussars. He greeted me with great emotion and excitement and told me his story. A machine gun bullet had struck the side of his head and destroyed his sight. The German surgeons had extracted the bullet and were now awaiting tests to see if Billy's sight would recover. We continued to swap our experiences and ignored the frantic waving of hands from the wounded Germans and the fact that the sister in charge had found my bed empty and was about to find me. She smacked me on the right bottom, lifted me up, muttering all the time, and carried me back to my bed and my pulley.

Shortly after, we saw through the glass roof of the hospital our fighter planes and they rained down pamphlets which apparently told of the imminent battle for this area and that time would be given for the evacuation of the hospital. We were to become the front line. This proved to be the case, as shortly afterwards our fighter planes and bombers flew overhead and the hospital was ordered to be cleared. So we were all taken to the railway and were packed into various carriages and horse trucks to begin what proved to be a very long and difficult journey into central Germany.

The wounded were lying about and there were eight cattle trucks to take us, converted to carry stretchers. There was no medical officer on the train that I knew of, just Red Cross men who moved about and gave us drinks. At one point the train stopped and we were told that those who could move could get off the train and go into a hut where there would be plates of sauerkraut for us to eat. I couldn't move but some of them got out but couldn't eat the food, so they boarded the train and on we went. The train went very slowly and although there were tin pails for toilets on the train many men were able to step off the train as it was moving and did their business outside. Next to my bunk was the blinded Billy Watson.

WALTER HUMPHRYS

We were put in a field in a wire cage with buckets of water where we spent the night. In the morning, Uhlans marched us to Caudry where we were sorted out into Divisions. Here, two Germans lined us up and as we passed them, one took our helmet off and the other put a civilian hat on us. They had evidently got these from civilian places they'd taken over, all sorts of hats, panamas, straw hats and lord knows what. Then as they lined us up again, a German came along and told us to turn all our pockets out and put the things into a sack. Afterwards we were stripped, and told to stand in front of a German officer, while a private and a sergeant pointed out all our identity marks, scars, blemishes and such like so that we'd be recognised again if we tried to escape. A dinner of a kind of horse beans was given to us and we slept in barracks before going on the next day by train to Le Quesnoy, where we spent another couple of days in open fields, being supplied with food which, despite hunger, many could not eat.

After two or three days, we found our way back to Bellicourt at about 3am on the 30th, that was where the canal comes out between St Quentin and Cambrai, into the Hindenburg line there. For the next three or four weeks we slept in a barn with little or no roof, herded together like cattle and in a very dirty state as there were no facilities for washing or cleaning.

BILL EASTON

After being over-run by waves of German soldiers, Bill had only to wait quietly until mopping up parties returned to take him prisoner. Joining the rest of the POWs, he began to walk back through the German lines.

We were formed up when all of a sudden a young, scruffy-looking fellow caught me such a bang in the back with his rifle butt, I nearly fell down. I swore at him. These Germans, they never spoke to you, if they wanted anything it was the rifle butt, and my goodness that hurt you. He said to me, 'Cavalry'. I said, 'No'. Bang! He had two or three goes at me before I was hauled away in front of an officer. This officer was about the same age and he began yelling at me, banging on the wall, stamping, shouting out 'Cavalry, Cavalry' and I said, 'No!' And this little devil, he gave me another jab. I could hardly stand. Then the officer said, 'Artillery.' Again I said, 'No,' but I knew what he was getting at. I had come from the 25th Division and its divisional sign was a red horseshoe. It was a sign I wore on the rear of my tunic, whereas all the men from the Norfolks had yellow oblong and square patches sewn on their backs. I told him I was in the RAMC, when there was a calm voice behind me, honestly it was like a comedy, and somebody said, 'You are in trouble. He doesn't like you, old chap.' I said, 'I don't like him a lot either,' and this voice said, 'He can't speak English, what's the problem?' The voice then spoke German to the officer, I don't know what he said. I looked round and saw a high-ranking officer like you see in a caricature, he was dressed up to the nines, he'd a monocle, a stick and a cigar. I said, 'He thinks I'm cavalry.' 'I know you're not cavalry, you're 25th Division. What are you doing down here? You are about the only one of your lot. I've been all the way down this front these last two or three days, and I haven't seen any from your Division. Where are they now?' I told him I didn't know. 'I was sent here and I don't know why.' 'Oh well, it's quiet out there now,' he said, and I replied, 'It wants to be!'

This other officer was still shouting but I suppose he must have been told to shut up because he went silent all of a sudden. A minute or two later, this caricature spoke again. 'I'll tell you what. I'll get my man up here and I'll show this officer a chart.' A whistle was blown and a man rushed in and saluted before disappearing, only to return with a metal tube. This high-ranking officer took the end off the tube and produced a linen chart on which was printed every divisional sign of the British army. 'Here you are,' he said, and there was mine as large as life. I looked at it and agreed. 'Now his lordship will kick up a row. He's going to be very annoyed, and he's going to take it out on you,' this German told me. I thought to myself, 'Yes, he'll bring a rifle and give me the butt two or three times.' I wasn't looking forward to it, so he said, 'Come here a minute.' He spoke to the other officer and then told me in English, 'I can't order him to let you go, but while I show him this chart, you had better slide off, now you have the chance.' So I left the dugout and dropped-in with the hundreds of other prisoners who were passing by and that was the last I saw of him.

We marched from four that afternoon until late evening and it rained like the devil. It was cold, dark, and as we walked along, there were hundreds of us, I suppose, and if one man fell down you had to leave him, they wouldn't let you pick him up. Eventually we were taken to a field, where some workers came and put barbed wire around us, and as we would stop there until next day, we should lie down. The ground was as wet as anything; we were drowned rats, cold, but they told us anyone who got up would be shot.

CHAPTER THREE

Behind Enemy Lines

Not all soldiers who were captured were sent to prisoner of war camps in Germany. During the war, a small number of prisoners on all sides were kept in France to be used as cheap labour, carrying supplies, building and repairing roads, or working in forestry. There were rules which governed this labour, the major belligerents agreeing that men should not be employed in jobs directly connected with the war effort, such as digging trenches or carrying ammunition, nor were they meant to be employed within thirty kilometres of the front line. There was a principle that a prisoner could not, and indeed should not, be expected to work against the interests of his own nation. Equally, there was a common interest in reducing the chance of prisoner death or injury to an absolute minimum. However, despite the high-minded aims, both sides widely employed prisoners and, on many occasions, deliberately broke the rules.

In the world's first total war, almost all jobs could be deemed as helpful to the enemy. While helping to transport ammunition was clearly in breach of the regulations, many labouring jobs fell into a grey area. Simply mending roads could be construed as war work if it helped enemy transport arrive more efficiently at the front. Similarly, felling trees could be deemed war work, irrespective of whether the wood was used to keep soldiers warm or made into duckboards to line the bottom of a trench.

There is little evidence that the authorities worried too much about these borderline areas. All sides could not help contravening the rules. However, there were occasions for anger when prisoners were found to be working too close to the enemy lines. One such public incident led the Germans to transfer 500 British prisoners to the Russian front as a direct reprisal for the British employing German prisoners too close to the line. Many did not to survive this ordeal.

As war weariness set in, the Germans, in particular, became ever more desperate to win. The Allied naval blockade on Germany, and their own economic mismanagement, had created enormous shortages at home. While the German Army had first call on the nation's industrial and agricultural output, it became increasingly clear to the German High Command that an offensive in the west must split the Allies and finish the war quickly. The use of prisoners at the front became vital to the German war effort so that all available forces could be directed to, and maintained at, the front during the campaign. This over-riding aim ensured that the number of British prisoners employed at the front rose dramatically after the Spring offensive of 1918. Not only were thousands of prisoners captured in the first weeks of the offensive kept in France but other prisoners, already living in camps in Germany, were transferred back to the Western Front. By the Armistice, it was estimated that as many as a sixth of all British prisoners were working in France or Belgium.

Unlike prisoners in Germany, many of whom had been receiving parcels from regimental aid committees and latterly the Red Cross, the prisoners in France typically received little or nothing. As they moved around the battle zone, their whereabouts were unknown to the authorities back home. Some men missing, presumed killed, were later found to have survived and were working in France; others will have died there, the manner of their death, from over-work, illness or starvation, at odds with the accepted belief that it was on the battlefield. Even when word was passed to Britain that a certain private was alive and working in France, the chance of his receiving a parcel was low. Camps did exist, but many of the prisoners were held in former French prisons, in the cellars of fortified towns or simply sleeping in guarded farm houses and barns. Here men survived on the scraps from the foodstuffs sent to the front for the German army, food which was pitifully poor in the first place. Otherwise they survived on what they could steal or scrounge. Men learnt the tricks of the trade quickly, such as jostling for an outside position in the ranks of marching men. This way there was always the hope of picking up a discarded cigar end, plucking a vegetable from the roadside verge or being the recipient of some morsel of food quickly handed over by a passing civilian.

As the German offensive faltered and then failed, prisoners were forced to make the arduous journey from village to village, following the German army as it fell back in the summer and autumn of 1918. Sleeping rough, these prisoners were often subject to arbitrary discipline and cruel punishment, as guards, under stress and bitter at defeat, abused and neglected them. As the wave of Spanish flu hit Europe in 1918, prisoners succumbed in their hundreds. In the end, an unknown number of POWs died in France, many being buried when they fell. One corporal was later to estimate that of the 2,000 men captured with him in May 1918, only 292 accompanied him into captivity in Germany five months later.

ERNIE STEVENS

We were in a large field surrounded by barbed wire up on posts, herded into this cage. I got away from the entrance as soon as I could, for every five minutes or so these gates would open and in came more prisoners. There were no tents, or bedding, nothing at all for hundreds of prisoners. We just had to lie on the ground and sleep as best we could as the cage got more and more crowded; the Germans seemed to be capturing whole battalions of men. While we sat there we were allowed to fill out a card saying that we were prisoners, that we weren't wounded. I know it took about five or six weeks to reach my mum. It must have been horrible for her waiting for news, a terrible burden, I realised that, but there was nothing I could do.

The next day, a number of us were collected and taken out of the cage to a dump near the railhead. We were told to pick up boxes of machine gun ammunition unloaded from the trucks and follow a German soldier back towards the line close to where the Germans had advanced. I knew that we were NOT, according to the conventions of the time, to have anything more to do with the war. We knew it was wrong, we'd had lectures on war conventions before we ever left for France. At meetings, a senior officer would appear and given us information about what we should do and what we shouldn't do if we were taken prisoner, and it's something I enjoyed and heartily approved of. But we knew, 'Okay, you don't want to carry it? Here's a bullet.' Nobody wanted to be killed, I mean it's as plain and simple as that. We knew that would happen and we knew the Germans didn't care a tinker's cuss, just so long as the job was done the way they wanted it done. Was I angry? I wasn't happy about it, no. As we carried these boxes near a place called Laventie, we passed a field. In it we could see any number of Portuguese all lying on their faces, facing the rear. They had evidently been caught unawares and mown down by the attacking Germans.

On the second day in the cage, we were taken out to carry timber but on the third we didn't have much to do. By this time there was hardly room to lie down in the cage, so many men had come in. Then, shortly after, we were lined up and taken for a long walk to a railway where we were locked into cattle trucks and taken to the Citadel at Lille before moving on by train to Germany.

BILL EASTON

Under threat of being shot if they stood up, Bill and the other POWs spent most of a cold and wet night lying out beneath the stars.

At four in the morning, I heard a voice ask, 'Any Field Ambulance men who would like to do their comrades a good turn, come to the wire.' I went, and this German said, 'We have got a lot of wounded in the church and we can't look after them because we haven't got enough men and we've got our own people to look at.' There were about twenty ambulance men in the cage, and I thought, 'Oh somebody'll do it', but none of them volunteered. I thought, 'That's a good advert for the RAMC,' so I said that I would go. I was taken by a friendly sergeant who could speak English. He took me to a big church in which there were a few candles flickering, and a couple of poor hurricane lamps burning. He said, 'You'll find a good supply of water here, and I'll see you in the morning.' I nearly had a fit. There were men lying in the pews and there were men lying right up the main aisle, none on stretchers, just lying all on the floor. I couldn't see and I had to go and bend over, only to find out that some of them must have been dead when they were taken in there. I went round and found that a lot of the chaps in the aisle were dead, they'd been there a couple of days. I made my way up the aisle towards the altar and I sat there and I tell you, I thought to myself, 'You always were a mug.' It was then that I thought I could hear somebody talking. There was quite a space near the pulpit and a dim glow from some candles, so I walked over and I could see faces, and do you know, when I counted there were just on forty men there with mostly light wounds in the shoulders and arms. I gave a drink to those I found alive. Funny thing, the wounded weren't concerned with their drink so much, those wounded chaps who had blood on their hands were most keen to get their hands washed. I'd

Thomas Spriggs at 103; before he died in January 2001 he was the last prisoner taken during the German counter-offensive at Cambrai, November 1917.

A rare image taken by a German photographer of British POWs doubling back after capture near Armentières, 10th April 1918. It is noticeable that the foreground is in focus and not the soldiers, giving the impression that this was a hastily taken snapshot. IWM Q48376

George Gadsby, August 1999

George Gadsby, front right, before he went to France. He is with his father and three brothers.

30th March 1918. The King talks to Private Denny and the remainder of the 7th Sherwood Foresters at Hermin, after the Battle of Bullecourt. Jack Rogers' battalion had suffered over 95 per cent casualties, killed, wounded, and taken prisoner, on the 21st March 1918. IWM Q295

Die deutsche Verteidigungs-Offensive im Westen.
Rast engl. Gefangener vor dem Abtransport nach der Sammelstelle.

7767

British officers are photographed by a German war photographer. Their depression at capture and their utter fatigue are clearly etched on their faces.

Bill Easton, sitting, prior to going to France in 1917.

British NCOs and other ranks congregate in a holding cage after capture. The heap of gas masks is testimony to their number.

Die deutsche Verteidigungs-Offensive im Westen.
Eintreffen der ersten englischen Gefangenen in einer Sammelstelle bei St. Quentin.

A remarkable picture of British prisoners arriving in Germany, filthy and clearly battle worn. The journey might take over two days and was often made without a break.

A letter written from the front by a friend of Bill Easton's informing Bill's mother of her son's disappearance. He is keen to reassure her that Bill is probably a prisoner of war and not dead.

The card filled out by Ernie Stevens and sent to his mother. Ernie's mother, Mrs Philpotts, had remarried after Ernie's father was killed in the Boer War.

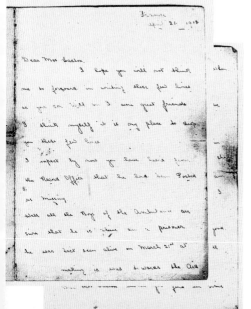

deutsche Verteidigungs-Offensive im Westen.

Ein engl. Gefangener vor dem Abtranspo
nach der Sammelstelle.

Men filling out a card which will be sent to England informing loved ones of their capture.

British prisoners lying in a church. The Germans have thoughtfully provided straw and blankets for the men.

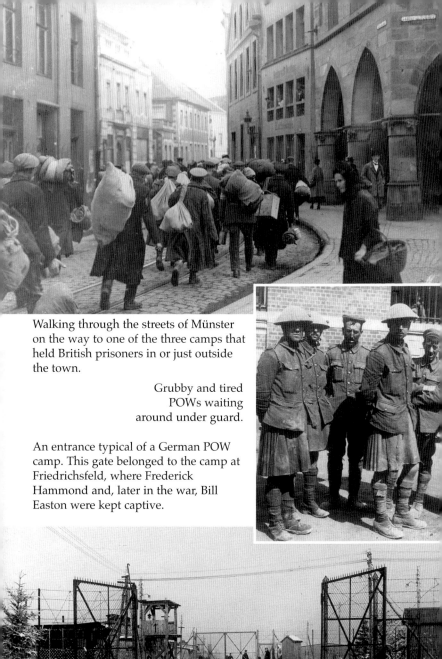

Walking through the streets of Münster on the way to one of the three camps that held British prisoners in or just outside the town.

Grubby and tired POWs waiting around under guard.

An entrance typical of a German POW camp. This gate belonged to the camp at Friedrichsfeld, where Frederick Hammond and, later in the war, Bill Easton were kept captive.

Tightly packed beds in a British POW barracks in a camp at Münster. Sleeping accommodation was often at a premium, so that soldiers slept close together as in this picture, or in lines of bunk beds.

A British POW is buried. The makeshift coffin is reasonably solid and better than many that were used.

British and French prisoners arriving at Münster III, the buildings of which exist to this day.

Football is played at Münster III where is now a car park.

Other entertainment included amateur productions. This card, picked up at a postcard fair, turned out to show the father of the author's neighbour. He is Corporal Alfred Horrix of the 2nd Suffolks (front left) who was captured at Le Cateau.

Early exponents of the pole vault compete at Münster III.

The notorious Karl Niemeyer, the brutal commandant of Hölzminden Camp. IWM Q69488

A plan of Dülmen, as the camp existed between 1914 and 1921. After the war, the camp was briefly used as a repatriation camp for returning German POWs. The entrance would have been close to the roadway at the bottom of the picture.

After 1921, the camp was dismantled and the grounds returned to the landowner. This wall, one of the few remains, was part of the German guards' canteen at Dülmen Camp (circled as no 4 in the Deutsches Lager).

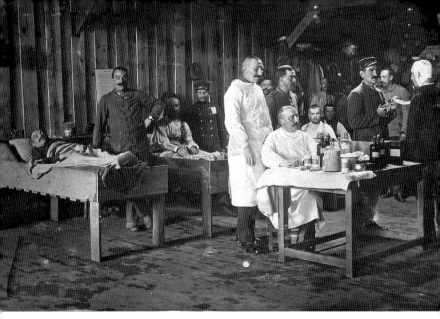

German doctors (although in reality they were more often captured medical orderlies) help dress the wounds of a POW. The sparse surroundings reflect the fact that most hospitals were simply barracks.

These British prisoners were held at Doberitz Camp and were sent down a salt mine every day. Note the heap of salt behind the men.

Many German civilians were kind to POWs. Leni Mörrs, a hotellier befriended Bill Easton, while Frierich Rosen was considerate to Ernie Stevens when both men worked at a soda factory.

Wooden clogs being made by prisoners for prisoners at Münster II. It was in a room like this that Jack Rogers worked with a Frenchman called Roget in 1918.

A panorama of Münster III. This POW camp had been an army barracks pre-war and had been built to a very high standard. As a result it was far more comfortable than the other camps in the vicinity.

The camp as it appeared in January 2000. The entire area of the barracks had become a building site with each house being turned into modern flats and the land in the middle used for car parking. The buildings to the right were already renovated while the buildings ahead and to the left were due for renovation.

The orchestra at Dülmen camp. It is said that the instruments arrived in the camp at the behest of the commandant, who also gave permission for a 600 seater theatre to be built. Several members of the Paris Opéra were held captive at the camp and performances were always 'sold out'.

(Right & below right) Prisoners with time to spare went to extraordinary lengths to produce costumes. Pictures such as these show that many camps were well run and that some commandants acted in a humane and benevolent way.

Jack Rogers, on the left, acting in a play at Münster I in 1918.

never had that happen before. I'd got buckets of water there and I spent my time going round trying to clean them up.

In the morning, the main doors of the church flew open and a German sergeant came in. He'd got an escort of four soldiers who passed by him, about turned, banged their rifles on the floor, then shouldered arms. After a lot of ritual stamping about, the sergeant saluted me. I thought, that's a funny thing, saluting a prisoner. Then he said, 'I'm speaking on behalf of my colonel, who wishes to thank you very much.' He then said, 'With our job we can't afford to be bitter enemies. Do you feel my bitter enemy?' I told him that I had no personal animosity against him. We shook hands and he told me not to think of him as an enemy: he couldn't have been nicer.

He told me that there were quite a lot of supplies coming up in lorries and that the lorries were going back empty. They were going to pick up German casualties at one end of the village but the transport was going to pass right by the gates of the church and a certain section would stop and pick up the wounded. There was a railhead about ten miles behind the lines, and would I be in charge of getting those wounded who could move onto the lorries. I said, 'I'm sure I can manage it,' but when I saw the first lorry I nearly fainted. I could stand there and look into the back of the lorry and the floor board nearly came up to my eyes, a good five foot high and I thought to myself, 'Cor, we've got to lift somebody up there!' Each lorry had a driver and a deputy and over the course of the next day I helped to evacuate these British soldiers down the line. These drivers were very good to our men. They had cigarettes and, do you know, nearly all the wounded were given a smoke, although the German cigarettes were by that time as rank as anything.

I was given permission to accompany the last of the wounded down to the railhead, but when I got there and the wounded were unloaded, I was ignored. Everyone just carried on and I was left standing there until a German came up and I was taken to a canteen for some food. After a while,

I was approached by a German sergeant, who said, 'I have a request. If you agree, we are allowed to keep POWs close to the front to help with the wounded.' The German medical service's motto was 'The wounded always come first', they used to quote it to me, and they needed as much help as they could get. There was a hospital being opened about four miles from the line, and I consented to stop and help. On the 25th of March I wrote in Sergeant Charley Feldner's diary the following: 'This is to certify that I, William Easton, do, quite voluntarily, proceed within thirty kilometres of the front with the 625th Sanitäts Komp.'

GEORGE GADSBY

After his death-defying attempts to escape captivity, George had finally been surrounded and taken prisoner; his battalion had been virtually wiped out. For the next nine months he was to remain in France and Belgium.

We entered Cambrai on the 12th of April and were escorted into a high walled enclosure, peacetime barracks for a French garrison. On the following Monday, we were turned out at 6.30am and placed in small parties ready for work. Nineteen of my comrades and myself eventually arrived at a large dye works where our job consisted of smashing up machinery. We were disgusted at having to break up such valuable engines so as to reduce them to scrap iron. Had we refused, however, our food would have been reduced and we could ill afford this as we were already in a state of semi-starvation. The majority of us that morning came out to work with just a drink of 'camouflaged coffee' made from burnt barley, having eaten our bread ration the previous day.

Soon after, our labours were transferred to a very large sugar refinery. It was so large that 400 prisoners could hide themselves in its gigantic boilers and engines. It reminded one more of a game of hide and seek, for every time the sentry came near, one of our number would give a bang with our chisel or strike with a hammer to make a noise with whatever happened to be in our possession. Their supervision only consisted of minute visits and during many of my days there the result of a day's labour amounted to an unbolted screw. We did not do any work if we could possibly avoid it and every opportunity we got of smashing tools without arousing the attention of the Germans, we did so.

It was not always so easy. On another occasion in a cotton factory under a villain of a German, two of my comrades and I had to use a sledgehammer alternately with unceasing vigour from 7am until 2pm. It was not a pleasant pastime hammering with our scanty physical energy at a piece of iron. Another phase of collecting scrap iron was taking down iron gates and railings. It did not matter whether they belonged to rich or poor unless some high-ranking German officer inhabited one or more of the rooms when probably they would be allowed to remain. Later, it became necessary for the Germans to think about transporting the iron to the furnaces, and so we were employed loading it up into various means of transport including a motor-van, a steam tractor and even teams of oxen. We worked at the station but on many mornings our party lay down in the yard, as trucks very seldom came to be loaded owing to the fact that the Germans had very few wagons to spare. It became evident that much of the iron would never reach Germany. We were already receiving news that our comrades were advancing rapidly, and the noise caused by the exploding shells became louder and louder.

There was always a big rush to form up, for this kind of employment was very pleasant, we being able to obtain news from the French civilians and generally obtain a little food which was smuggled to us.

BILL EASTON

Working with a German medical unit was highly irregular. Bill realised, however, that as he was a prisoner, helping all the wounded must now be his priority.

There were no ambulances so a train was brought up to take the wounded away. It was like a miniature train with a tiny little motor, petrol driven, and was manned by what were known as Freiwillige. These were boys aged up to about fifteen who could volunteer for service but weren't allowed closer than ten miles from the line. They were a boisterous lot. I'd seen them build this small gauge line, carrying the rails, some twenty foot long. The train had open trucks with back to back seats facing towards and away from the engine. They could shift hundreds of men quickly and were mostly for the lightly wounded, so that should these trains be derailed they could take the wounded off and lift the trucks back on to the line.

I'd wanted some men to help me load the wounded onto the train but Charley Feldner came back and said that he'd spoken to four men who came from the Midlands and that they'd said they were not going to help no bloody Germans. Two of them said they might but this other fellow, a big chap, he swore and had told them they would be shot for helping. Charley came and asked me if I would have a word with them. I went and saw them and asked what they had against helping to evacuate the wounded. However, this big fellow said, 'We're not all German lovers, you can go and help them but you won't get any help from us.' There was a hell of a row, and he swore at me, calling me everything but a Christian. I told them that the job was really nothing to do with the Germans and that I only wanted a bit of help to get those fellows away. I asked one of the others what he thought but he pretty much repeated that of course I was helping them. I told them I would come back in half an hour. When I returned two of them were wavering and I mentioned that the Germans were picking men out for labour camps and if they didn't help me 'you'll go and lord help you if you do', so in the end I bulldozed them into helping.

I was nicknamed the Kleiner Engländer, the little Englishman, and I worked at this hospital under Charley Feldner. He was very good to me and called me William and spoke to me in beautiful English, having lived in America for some time. A lot of the men in the company came from Hamburg and pre-war there had been a sea link between Hamburg and Kings Lynn, my home town. Several had visited my town and could speak good English. A lot had the idea that the Germans were fighting the wrong country, that we should have turned on the French instead.

There was a sergeant major, Sub-Lieutenant Lindemann, there and he was a brute to his own men but he treated me marvellously. He always carried a thin cane and if a man passed, no matter which way he happened to be looking, if he didn't turn round and salute, Lindemann would cut him across the back of the neck with this cane so that I've seen them fall down. Every morning, about 11 o'clock, he'd shout at the top of his voice, 'Wilhelm', that was me, 'Kommen Sie mit,' 'come with me', so we'd go to the canteen and he'd order a flagon of beer. After a drink he'd get up and throw a note on the counter and he'd say, 'Wilhelm, pfennige', and the change would rattle on the counter and that was a sign for me to pick them up. Well, they weighed a blinkin' ton and I used to put them in my pocket until my pockets began to sag.

Honestly, we were friends and I worked among the Germans quite willingly, helping the wounded. I had been working there for a while when Charley, he seemed to run the show, came up to me and said, 'I have an invitation for you. It's not right that you should be here giving orders to men and you're not a sergeant, so while you're with us you'll be an acting sergeant.' Charley told me that, 'As a mark of respect, you'll be the guest of honour at our party.' The party was held in what seemed to be an old schoolroom. The Germans had managed to get together free casks of beer, and I was asked along where this whole blooming company toasted my health, they were shouting 'Wilhelm' and cheering and I don't know what. It was announced that as I was helping with this hospital that they were getting ready, they were making me an honorary sergeant. This meant I could ask one of these German orderlies to do something and they'd do it, and I thought to myself, 'Well, what a thing.' I was offered a beer but I never drank, because I was a teetotaller, but they said, 'Well, you'll have to have a photo taken,' and that's me outside and I've got a damn great pint of beer in my hand – just for show, and that's Charley Feldner with his hand on my shoulder. They made a real fuss of me and I had to sing a song for them.

I worked like a free man. I went into the Mess as a sergeant, and slept in the same room as them. By that time I'd come to respect the Germans, individually I mean, because they were so friendly. Oh, the month or so that I was with them, do you know, those fellows that were getting a few things from home, they'd bring me bits of food. Eventually I got dysentery and that put an end to my work near the front line. The Germans were frightened of anything infectious and so I was put on a lorry straight away – no argument – and that's the last I saw of them.

THOMAS SPRIGGS

After my capture at Cambrai I was taken by box van and deposited at a camp called Dülmen in Westphalia. We were there from the start of December until about the end of January, and in that time we did very little work, just sat around as far as I can remember. When it was cold we used to sit near a massive stove in the hut. I remember this German officer coming in one morning complaining, 'Some mens works and some mens works not.'

By February I was back in Belgium at a place called Péruwelz. A group of us were sent as general labourers, first of all working on the train tracks. In those days there used to be light railways running along the roads in Belgium and I went to work there, track adjusting, tamping the ballast, relaying lines. I knew we weren't supposed to do anything to help the German war effort, but I don't think I gave it a thought. You were set a job and I think I did it to the best of my ability. I should have got a clout if I'd refused. What else could you do, you couldn't refuse to do these jobs and it wasn't particularly hard work as I recall. As for sabotage, no, that never occurred to me. I was out there to try and keep living until I was released.

It was there that I dropped a rail on my foot and burst the nail nearly off the toe. I remember some people in a shop dressed and wrapped it up for me. I went to the Lazarett in Saint Amand and went to see the military doctor there and he looked at it and got a knife and pushed it under the toe nail, slit one side, slit the other, no anaesthetic, and then wrapped it up in a bit of paper. My God, it did make me sweat and I thought, 'I'm not going to say a word,' and I remember the sweat rolled off me with the pain. I had to walk back to Péruwelz from where we moved into some timber yards, at Raismes, where we unloaded planks and stacked them on trolleys for the saw mill. There were huts being made, and I remember once going back to the camp with a Prussian guard or 'postens' as we called them. He was a rather tall school-master, white headed, we used to call him Snowball. He'd picked about twenty of the taller men as his own squad. We'd got uniforms through the Red Cross by this time, blue with brown armbands and a broad band down the leg, and he loved to march us down the street to this timber yard, he was so proud. Coming back one day, we passed a convent and there was a brick wall chest high with boards above that and a little gap in between. Suddenly I saw a sandwich poke up between the wall and the board so I just stepped out, took the sandwich, popped it in my pocket and rejoined the ranks. Some days later the same thing happened but I was on the left hand side, marching. I remember there was a fellow there, he'd seen what had happened and he'd taken good care to be on the right hand side of our little squad. Sure enough, he saw this sandwich come up and he stepped out of rank, over the path, but the posten saw him and he soon got a rifle butt about his shoulders. He got a beating. And yet we were walking back along this road and there was an Irishman in our team called Paddy Shean, and coming towards us at some cross-roads was a fellow with a couple of horses and a wagon, and on this wagon was a tree trunk. As he turned the corner, somehow or other the trunk swung round and clipped Paddy, cutting his head a little bit, and my God didn't the posten get onto the driver of this horse, he did slate him.

WALTER HUMPHRYS

As part of our labour we had to recover old shells and iron, frequently meaning 6am to 12.30pm and from 1.30pm to 8pm. Occasionally we were turned out again at 10pm or later for a few hours' extra work, no allowance being made in our food ration the next day. From there we worked on roads, stone cracking and road repairing, as well as the railways. I was ill with dysentery at the time but was obliged to work, which instead of breaking my spirit, only intensified my hatred for the way we were treated.

Then we worked at laying an electric cable up across the Hindenburg line, over the barbed wire. It was here that I fell down a trench, my knee doubling underneath me as I landed kneecap first on a rusty barbed wire spike. I carried on working but I had a lot of trouble, my knee swelling to such a size that it was necessary to cut my trousers off. Cold fomentations were applied daily but my knee festered and festered and, in agony, I was eventually taken into a German hospital and they cut me open in the side and at the front of the knee and lanced the abscesses. They had no cotton wool or linen, so they used paper bandages and it remained open all the weeks, cold fomentations being continually applied. I was well treated here, being given the same food as the wounded German soldiers on the ward. The German Sister did many little kindnesses for which I thanked her when leaving, some weeks later.

On returning to camp, I was employed stripping leaves off nettles, tying the stems in bundles and packing them to be sent to Germany to be made into cloth. The next week was spent sawing wood and carrying water to the cookhouse. From September, work consisted of digging out old iron from trenches and loading it upon wagons which we then pulled back to camp. Other jobs at this time included a fortnight working on the railways at Le Cateau, tapping the stones underneath the sleepers, then another fortnight working with another man sawing railway sleepers with a double handed saw.

For much of the time we stayed in a big farmhouse by the side of a road. It was a compound, not a prison camp. One building was the guards' billet, and the rest of the buildings were segregated off with high barbed wire, isolating the stables and a couple of the barns behind it. We worked on the stables, as this was where we slept, turning out all the horse tackle. Six sloping wooden platforms were erected which accommodated about ten men sleeping side by side. Here we lay under two blankets and in the clothes we worked in. We also had a string towel, enamel bowl, spoon and a pair of wooden clogs. These we put in a sandbag, wrapped in a tunic, and that was our pillow. The stable windows were all boarded up and there was no light or heat. We had a cold water standpipe with half a barrel underneath and that was to wash in. There was no soap, except a kind of powder they gave us, but nobody used it as it skinned your face.

Throughout the whole period of captivity, it was the

custom to issue the ration of bread at teatime for the following day. Most of us were so hungry that invariably we ate it all for tea and then went to work next morning without any breakfast. I usually went with two others to the back of the barn and, sitting on some bricks, we made a fire with wood, very often boiling our bread in a quart of acorn coffee making an unpalatable but filling meal.

From October, we retired with the Germans. During this time, our boys came over and started bombing a place close by, so we were always under a certain amount of risk from aeroplanes but not from actual combat. On another occasion an aeroplane came over and dropped a bomb in the field by the side of us.

One evening a small party of us were taken by an officer to a railway siding where there were empty trucks. There were some shells nearby and he ordered us to load these into the wagons. I had sorted out and loaded up shells before, unwillingly, but this time one fellow, an older man, said we shouldn't do it, 'It's against international law.' So we said we wouldn't do it. This officer said that if we didn't, he would shoot us. We had another dis-cussion and said we wouldn't load them. In the end he didn't say anything, he just marched us back to the compound, French prisoners being used to do the work instead.

BILL EASTON

I was taken to a hospital near Condé, picking up two other men on the way. The journey was terrible, banging up and down all the way. The hospital was part of an old French prison and the three of us were taken in and laid on the floor, one on each side of me. I was very ill and felt as if I was finished. I couldn't speak or do anything. They took the man on the right away and I thought they were putting him to bed. And then a little while after, they took the other man away.

Waiting for my turn, I heard somebody say, 'I thought there were three of them.' 'Oh,' said a Scottish voice, 'Two of them snuffed it right away – they're only waiting for him to go.' That was me! As I laid there, a chap came across and gave me a drink and said to me, 'What's that fool been saying?' I told him that the two men beside me had died and that I would be next. 'Oh, I've told him to clear off, he's a proper pessimist,' he said. He was a sergeant and he told me he had been training to be a doctor before he'd volunteered to fight and been captured about the same time as me. They used to give men opium for dysentery and he said that the Germans had developed a substitute only a third as strong, but would I trust him to administer it to me. He'd tried it on a couple of people before and they'd come round.

Dysentery, well, it's just as if your inside is running out of you, anything you take goes straight through you. You want to die and every so often you're out of this world and then you come back again and then you have another dose of it until you're so weak that you die. They gave us something called Pammus, it was something ground up and tasted horrible and I was always sick with it straight away. I was also given some stuff like paste you put on a wall, that was supposed to have opium in, again it made me sick but this sergeant told me that would wear off, and it was true and within a few weeks I was mobile again.

The Germans weren't letting anybody in unless they were really ill. Even so there were half a dozen camps around Condé and the sick were coming into the hospital every day. There were beds all over the place. As I was getting better I noticed something funny. I asked one of the men, 'How is it you've got all these people, nearly every bed's got an Orderly?' I discovered that a scam was being worked in the hospital. Men were going sick and, playing on the fear the Germans had of anything contagious, they were getting into hospital, after which the Germans wouldn't come anywhere near. These people were sent in with their records and they kept them a while, then they were 'killed off', but they weren't all dead, they were working in the hospital.

Nevertheless, a lot of men were dying in there from dysentery. These they used to bury by the dozen in coffins that reminded me of orange crates, you could see through the wood. They used to have some people from a medical college and they used to do post mortems. They used to cut them open but nobody wanted to sew them up again. At the front, the Germans didn't have much in the way of bandages. Mostly they had some adhesive and they'd put a bit round the wound and stick a bit of paper on. Anyway, we got hold of some of that and instead of sewing up the bodies, those who were on some punishment or other were made to go down early in the morning and use this adhesive and paper. These students used to cut the bodies to pieces sometimes and there were these plasters all over them. I mean, we were supposed to sew them back up but the Germans didn't mind. After that, an old Frenchman used to come with some men and women and they used to clean the bodies, put them in the boxes, record their names, lay a paper shroud over them and nail the coffins down. We had to get up early and there would be a row of dead and we would put them on a hearse crossways, about eight to ten on there, right high. The old horse that pulled the hearse looked as though it was going to fall down every minute. We'd be going along and that old horse would stop all of a sudden for a breather and it's a wonder the blinkin' coffins didn't fall off. We used to have to go just outside the gate and this podgy German, I think he was Roman Catholic, he would waddle along and he used to read and chant all the way down to the cemetery with those who were the bearers – those who were mobile – walking behind. On the way, we'd pass some cottages and the women, they used to come out there, on their knees, and the old Father would stop the procession and bless them. There was a trench dug as far as you could see across this field, deep enough to take two coffins on top of one another, and he'd say a little service. Oh, I used to hate that job, to see this trench going practically out of sight and you know you were going to fill that in, I didn't like that at all. Occasionally if we had more than eight dead, the hearse would go back and another squad would load them up and we'd still be there. Then the Priest would say his litany, none of us could understand, then he would say 'Erde, erde', and we'd have to put a handful of soil on each coffin before we shovelled the earth into the trench. He was ever so particular, was this old boy, that it was done right. He used to shake the water over each coffin, but once he'd finished, all of a sudden he'd turn round and try to get us to hurry. Well, we couldn't, we'd got about two foot of earth to put on top of these coffins. Then on the way back, he used to recite something, God knows what it was, of course we were mostly younger fellows, we didn't trouble, we wanted to get rid of him, but he'd stand there and watch us until we got back into the gate.

I don't know if there was any way of identifying the bodies afterwards because it was quite chaotic. I suppose the names would be reported from that prison hospital as dead and those names would be sent on to the War Office, but there were no graves in the cemetery with names on. I was usually on the left of the burial party and one day as we passed some French people, one of them, a girl, said something to me and gave me a stick of bread. From then on, this girl, she would stand right close to the road and, every now and again, she used to bring one of these loaves and I'd tuck it under my coat. Once we were in the precincts of the hospital the Germans never took any notice of us, they didn't like getting too close.

One day the doctor told me that the only way I'd get to stay in the hospital was if I worked with infectious diseases. He told me the Germans had sent a man in who they said had got diphtheria. I was shown this man and I looked down his throat and the doctor asked me what I thought. I said, 'It looks like he's drunk something that has scorched his throat because it's brilliant red, but it's not diphtheria because there's no green streaks.' I told the doctor I had taken an exam in the Field Ambulance in England and diphtheria was one of the pictures they had shown me. This lad was called Kelly and he'd only got a sore throat but he and I were isolated for a few weeks in one wing of the place, sharing his Red Cross parcels that he received.

Eventually some one gave the game away, the Germans came in and cleared the whole place and a number of us were picked out to be sent to a labour company, or a punishment unit as I saw it. About twelve of us were sent to work loading and unloading a lime kiln. We were in a clearing in a wood and we used to have to barrel these big blocks of limestone into a kiln and then pile no end of timber on the top and let it burn for about three days. Then they'd open the kiln up and all this stuff had gone to lime, quicklime, and we had to shovel that out. It was red hot and it was put in heaps to cool before it was put into bags to go to Germany. It doesn't sound much, but I had a recurrence of dysentery and was in a state. I wasn't fit to walk, let alone being capable of hard work and the guards, they were brutes. The first thing they'd do, they'd rush out with a bang in the back with their rifles. Some of the fellows there were older than me, some of them were rough characters and some of them had been through the mill and they'd keep an eye on me. They called me the kid and if there were signs that one of these guards was approaching, they'd get round me. I was supposed to wheel this quicklime but I couldn't push the barrow and you'd go round a corner and one would stand there and if he felt like it, he would take a swipe at you as you went past. These older men, we stuck together and when they selected so many of us to go to Germany, we were almost like a club. If they scrounged anything, they'd share it with you. What we ate sometimes I don't know, but that was comradeship.

WALTER HUMPHRYS

I was hit once for warming my hands on the radiator of a lorry. It was very, very cold and we were lined up in a queue and I put my hand on the -radiator of the lorry to warm and an officer hit me on the shoulder with an ash cudgel of some sort, a fairly substantial thing. We weren't regularly hit but I mean if you'd been in the trenches that was nothing, if you've been in the trenches, you'd seen hell. You were so inured to everything, you were bloomin' hardened. It wasn't normal practice. Attacks depended on the guard, I mean a Saxon was more like a Somerset man, but if you got a Prussian then he was very military. The Germans varied a lot.

BILL EASTON

We had been working in a glass factory and we were moved. We did a hell of a walk that day and we went along a canal bank. On one side the ground had been cultivated and as they walked along, the men had eaten leaves of cale, like cabbage leaves. This was reported to the colonel and when we got to a village, there were about forty of us and no end of guards, we were paraded in the village square. This colonel was on a balcony of a hotel and they were serving him dinner as we stood there, watching. Then the in-terpreter got up and said that they had intended to give us a mid-day meal but owing to the behaviour of several miscreants – where he got that word from I don't know – the Colonel had decided we would not be fed. They would let us watch them eating as a punish-ment. And there they were, the colonel and a couple of officers, and they were toasting each other, holding up their glasses. That was punishment.

We went on and we came to another village near Mons and there was a row of cottages, five or six, on one side of the road. Evidently they were -civilians having an evening meal, perhaps they knew we were coming, because these women saw us there and they ran out with plates, with potato on. They ran in amongst us and do you know, the Germans halted us and they shouted out an order and the guards went and pushed the women away and then they went in and out of us smashing the plates with their rifle butts. I felt murderous. The food was on the floor and some of the chaps scrambled on the ground trying to eat it, but I think of these poor women, probably those were the only plates they'd got. God, there was some bitterness about that. These women were howling their heads off but we got the order to move and we left them crying over their bits of plates. We marched on another five miles or so where we camped in another barbed wire cage close to some regimental headquarters. It wasn't that secure, really, just a few strands round but nobody would have run away, they were too near dying. They never gave us a drink, they never gave us anything and I passed out, absolutely went right out. I woke to find some chap offering me some soup, where he'd got it from I'd no idea, but any rate I had it and felt much better. When I got up I asked him what was in that soup and he told me that there was a German rubbish heap up against the wire netting and the men had raked through all sorts of things to get the scraps. From there they'd boiled the lot up and I'd eaten it with relish.

The next morning we were back on our travels and I'm blowed if we didn't go back the way we'd come. Sometimes we'd march miles and miles and miles. Then, when it was evening, you'd be secured behind barbed wire and the guards would be having a nice feed opposite, right near you, and we'd never get anything. Sometimes they gave you something we called sandstorm, a yellow brew that was ground up maize or turnip. Its taste was horrible and sometimes you'd be sick all evening – but if you didn't have that, you didn't have anything.

CHAPTER FOUR

At the Kaiser's Pleasure

The number of Allied prisoners captured by the Germans during the First World War far exceeded their expectations. Initial battlefield success, particularly against the Russians and the French, drew in over 500,000 prisoners by Christmas alone. The British contingent, those captured in 1914, was, by comparison, small, around 19,500. However, owing to the unpreparedness of the Germans to handle such numbers, many of the first British prisoners in Germany had a torrid time, sleeping out in bell tents during a bitter winter while helping to build camps across Germany. In the end, some 200 parent camps were built, divided up into 21 Army Corps Districts, each district having its own almost autonomous commander, under whom each camp was run by an almost equally autonomous commandant. Attached to the parent camps were smaller camps, both supplying POW labourers to thousands of work kommandos. By the end of 1916 at least 970,000 prisoners were working in Germany either in industry or agriculture.

The camps varied in size but most parent camps housed certainly hundreds and often thousands of prisoners, packed into uniform huts, surrounded by barbed wire and watchtowers. Many were built in industrial areas so as to supply workers to the numerous steel works, soda factories, salt and coal mines, while other, smaller POW camps were built close to or between important industrial complexes so as to discourage Allied bombing. Long-range attacks had become a feature of the war in 1917 and 1918, as planes were built with a greater range and bombing capacity. It meant that even city councils, such as at Freiburg, voted to accommodate POWs in the town, using prisoners as a human shield against further Allied bombing.

In the confines of the camp, nationalities were generally segregated, areas of the complex rather than particular huts being designated as Russian, French or British. In some camps, prisoners of different nationalities barely spoke to each other, in others there was daily fraternisation. Language difficulties, particularly with the Russians, were normal but partially overcome, as one prisoner recalled. 'Daily contact was to become a quite normal matter; a quaint form of speech evolving from a mixture of words in French, German, Russian and English. Example: "I hear there is a big lot of French and Russians down for Kommando, Rusky: are you for it?" becomes the following: "Viel camarades for Kommando, tavarish, viel Franzosen, viel Rusky viel arbeit. You nix?" Rusky answers: "Ya ponessi. Me nix, me viele krank. Me rheumatiz. Viele krank, viel malade, nix arbeit, Kommando nix gut, nix essen alles Kaput." So I am told, "I want to keep off it, I'm sick, got rheumatics, very sick indeed. Can't work. Kommando kill you all off. Nothing to eat".' Such limited communication brought many POWs together in a temporary friendship, though all knew they would never see one another after the war.

Irrespective of nationality, the huts for the other ranks were spartan and generally cold, with perhaps one wood stove to heat the entire room. Bunk beds or tightly packed wooden cots were the norm, men sleeping on boards or wire netting with no more than one, possibly two, rough blankets under which to sleep. The rooms were cramped and, with barrack doors and windows closed by order at night, the air quickly became fetid. Such congested living conditions were not shared by the officers, who were generally more comfortable. They lived in huts or houses either in completely separate locations or in a different part of the camp, wired off from the area inhabited by the NCOs and men.

By convention, officers were not expected to work, nor were NCOs; even so, some did. The other ranks laboured around the camp, in the kitchens or washrooms or just outside if there happened to be any land on which to grow crops. Some camps were built close to the coalfields, as in the Ruhr and parts of Silesia, or near the salt mines as in the Hartz Mountains of central Germany. At these camps, men would be detailed to go down the mines, along with civilian workers, for shifts of up to ten hours a day. Others would be sent further afield to small camps, often no more than requisitioned hostelries or industrial buildings, where the men worked in local factories, foundries, or timber yards. The best jobs of all were working on the farms where men were fed better than anywhere else.

For officers the lack of work was often as much a trial as a privilege. Boredom was a great problem, although in camps such as those near the Black Forest, officers were allowed out for recreational walks once they had sworn on their honour, and in writing, not to escape. For those officers not so fortunate, as well as other ranks, there developed a mental condition known as barbed wire fever, an almost irrational feeling of claustrophobia. This was more prevalent at camps close to international boundaries, where the risk of a successful escape by prisoners ensured that security was much tighter.

Incarcerated for an unspecified time, men improvised. As well as the exist-ence of small libraries, camp magazines of notable quality were printed, often utilising the skills of former journalists and cartoonists. Elsewhere, football matches and athletic meetings were arranged, while camp entertainment, including remarkably well staged plays, was watched by hundreds of men at a time, anxious to forget their worries and desperate to pass the time. Amateur photographers, some French prisoners, but mostly Germans civilians, came to take pictures of the men, who spent what small amounts of camp money they were paid to have an image taken of themselves and made into postcards. These were either kept for posterity or sent home to their families. With the exception of photographic portraits, much the most common images are of prisoners participating in sports or in costume appearing on stage.

Images of smiling prisoners might reassure families at home and served as a good propaganda tool for the Germans, but they disguised the true nature of many soldiers' lives in the camps. Photographs hid the skinny legs and the ribs that poked through the skin. Arms might be painfully thin but in uniform they were not visible. Undoubtedly the food packages that arrived, helped revive those who were ill but the graves in the cemeteries that surrounded almost every camp gave the lie to the idea that these places were safe and comfortable. Some camps were good, some were bad, and some truly awful. The German authorities alone acknowledged that over 118,000 Allied prisoners died in their camps, particularly the Russians who received no outside assistance or help from home. Of course, many Allied prisoners died of wounds received on the battlefield, and some from illnesses that could not have been prevented. Many died of simple neglect, contracting diseases that might have been avoided had they not already been in a state of physical collapse.

And then there were those who were murdered, as some certainly were, as a direct or indirect result of a beating. Physical violence inflicted by an officer or NCO was anathema in the British Army, where even the mildest assault, if witnessed, could lead to a Court Martial and dismissal. In the British Army obedience was assured, if nothing else, by intimidation, whereas in the German Army the striking of junior ranks as a rebuke was generally tolerated. The Hague Rules had, in extreme circumstances, condoned the use of the rifle butt to ensure discipline but for prisoners in Germany any physical assaults, however mild, were shocking. As German prisoner of war camps were run largely independently of outside control, notions of discipline, if allowed free reign, could degenerate into brutal attacks. According to German figures, around four British soldiers a day died in German camps throughout the war, although none are recorded as having been as a result of physical attack. Official British figures put the number at around nine, with many deaths the result of an alleged assault. The true figure is not known but was certainly higher still.

NORMAN COWAN

After lying in a German hospital in Belgium, Norman, along with the other British prisoners, was evacuated from the fighting zone and sent on an arduous train journey into the heartland of Germany.

About halfway through the journey, the guards told us we were going to Saxony to a place called Quedlinburg in the Hartz Mountains. This dismal camp was situated outside a large village and had many compounds for British, French and Russians, of whom there were fewer but all starved and very neglected. The first impression I got was of a big tower and a man with a machine gun watching over the camp, although it wasn't closely guarded. We were about three hundred miles from anywhere, so it was perfectly feasible to walk outside the camp providing the men in the tower didn't see you. It was possible to escape, too, but nobody did that I was aware of.

The British compound was the largest in the camp, both in space and numbers. It was quite orderly and run by a committee of senior NCOs, many of whom had been captured during the various battles on the Marne and the Somme. We new arrivals at Quedlinburg were questioned by this group of NCOs. They seemed to be quite comfortable in the camp, as the German army custom was that their senior NCOs were not required to do any fatigue or guard duties and so over their long stay as POWs our men had gratefully adopted this system. All our NCOs and men had received regular Red Cross parcels to supplement the very meagre rations available from our German captors. However, those men who'd been captured at Mons, they were like fighting cocks. They had young Russian prisoners waiting on them. They never worked. They used to go dancing, dressed up like dolls. They didn't speak to you or mix with the other men and were quite -superior. They'd got uniforms, boots, everything from home and were living like lords.

BILL EASTON

Bill's health had all but collapsed. He had survived dysentery, hunger, physical attack and hard labour. Desperate to go anywhere rather than stay where he was, Bill was told that, for unspecified misdemeanors, he was to go to Germany.

An incident occurred one day, what happened I don't actually know, but afterwards we were taken to Condé and put into prison cells with just a slab of stone to sleep on, and grills where the door should have been. We were there three days before they told us we were being sent to Germany as a punishment. Before we boarded the train, they gave each of us a dried herring, half a loaf of bread and a bottle of water. This was supposed to last us the two-day journey but the bread, which was made from potatoes, turned sour in a day. Well, we were all hungry and ate the food and instead of two days we were three, nearer four, and of course we were starving. We arrived at Friedrichsfeld, a huge camp, and when we got out we did look a picture, we hadn't had a wash, we were scruffy and all of us stank to high heaven.

We were in a railway siding and next to us was a chewed up track which led right to the camp. Parallel to this track was a raised road, perhaps three or four feet higher than ours and as we walked along this track we could hear church bells being rung. We came round a corner and there were men dressed up in their best, there were women with blinkin' great hats on and as we came near them, these women started spitting at us and calling us swine and goodness knows what. Soon after, our track branched off. A few other prisoners had joined us on the train journey so there we were about fifty of us, all exhausted so that we had to be helped along until we went through the gate and into the camp.

JACK ROGERS

After barely surviving capture, Jack Rogers had been crammed into a cattle truck and sent to Germany. After a journey of two days, he had been only too glad to arrive.

We arrived at a town called Münster where there were three 'lagers' or prisoner of war camps, numbers one, two and three. We were for number one camp, and when we got out of these trucks, they brought round dixies full of some sort of ersatz coffee and a slice of brown bread. They formed us up to march through the town of Münster and you could see all the German people watching and I was surprised to see a good many of them were wearing wooden shoes. They weren't shouting, they were just looking, seeing all these different men going by in various uniforms, looking in awful condition, all dirty and wet and miserable. Germans with fixed bayonets escorted us to the camp. There was a big gate and then a guardroom through which we all had to pass. Beyond that, there was a grass centrepiece and all round this stood the huts. Each hut had a separate door and each was occupied by a different nation. Inside the huts were bunk beds made out of wood and chicken wire with one blanket per man. However, the blankets were outside the hut when we first arrived and it had begun to rain. So there we were on that first night, lying on a chicken wire bed under a wet blanket. And that's your lot, that's your home.

TOMMY GAY

The 'Great Push' on the Somme was to be the decisive attack that would hopefully win the war in 1916. Tommy Gay hoped – in vain – that his captivity would be short lived.

We were transferred to cattle trucks with just a sawn-off tub in the middle of the truck for a toilet and then sent to Germany, going through Cologne to Dülmen Camp, between Dortmund and Bochum. At Dortmund the truck was opened and we were given a shower. I remember there was a German fellow there with a tin of soft soap and he dipped his finger in the tin and splashed a bit of soap onto the head of each man as they walked by. They also gave us some potato water, because we did say to one another, as Englishmen, we said, 'I think this is the spud water where they've cooked some spuds for the sentries,' and we got a little basin full of that.

At Dülmen we lived in a barrack room full of bunk beds, with straw in each one to make them a bit more comfortable. We were given two blankets, one of which we lay on and the other one we lay under with our tunics on top as well. In the middle of the room there was a big iron stove to warm the barrack. Outside were the sentries, one every few yards, one here, one there, one there, all the way round the camp and that was nearly half a mile.

ERNIE STEVENS

Most of the guards were young guys who were not fit to go up the line, the dregs of the German population, whom they had to call up to look after -prisoners of war. We also had one or two elderly men who were very, very short tempered. There was one man we called Drippy because his nose always ran, he may even have been in his seventies and he was very nasty. We often used to see him sit down, just sit there against all regulations and after a time he would be snoring. We'd make a big bang every now and again to wake him up, just to annoy him. He'd swear at anybody and was not a man you could reason with in any way.

FRANK DEANE

Almost at the moment of capture, Frank had been wounded in the hand by a bullet. It was a light wound, but one that would ensure much-needed weeks of rest and recuperation.

I remember the first stop that particular night was at a place called Limburg, where we were turned out and given something to eat. I don't think I saw a German doctor because the one who dealt with me was a Russian orderly who was very good. I remember him rubbing a bit of iodaform right up my thumb, that was the most painful bit I had to put up with, and then it was just bandaged up with paper. Everything was made of paper then, what we would call toilet paper really, the bandages were made of woven paper as were the blankets and our hospital shirts. The bandages were slippery and would never stay on properly. The hospital was right next to the railway station, although it is a misnomer to call it a hospital, as it was an ordinary army hut, with just beds on either side. There I saw young fellows worse injured than I was, treated by a British doctor who was also a prisoner of war. It was a case of sorting out the needs of the patients, and those who were slightly injured or not in any danger had the less qualified orderlies. I did see one of our own doctors dealing with a young lad who'd had his hand and part of his forearm shot off and this doctor was pulling bits of broken bone out of it.

FREDERICK HAMMOND

We didn't have any German doctors, just Russians. Several men died in the camp, in hospital there. There was no medical treatment other than bandages in Germany. There was one fellow there with a broken arm and nothing was done to it at all and he could twist his arm round two or three times. Apart from my face I had also been wounded in the hand, three fingers. This hand became very swollen and they thought I might lose it at one time before a Russian doctor lanced it and it gradually got better.

But my worst injury was to my jaw. I had a bandage on my face, paper bandages, like crêpe paper, and for a long time, for more than a year afterwards, splinters of bone kept working their way out. I was getting better, but every time I went to eat I got a pain in the side of my face and my jaw would crack and tiny little splinters used to prick through the gum. Because my jaw had been smashed, I used to have to push the food through my teeth to eat because I could hardly open my mouth. I had to chew somehow and swallow, it was hard work.

ERNIE STEVENS

After his humiliating capture and enforced war work, Ernie was not sure what to expect when he finally reached Germany by train. In the event, he was quickly selected to join a work kommando near the town of Rheinberg. He was to stay there and work for the rest of the war.

At Dülmen, much information pertaining to our units and numbers and such like were taken down and put into a book.

Then, after one or two nights we were sorted out and in my case I was sent on a train with nearly forty others down to a German town called Rheinberg to a factory called the Deutsche Solvey-werke. There we joined about the same number of French and fifty or sixty Russians. There were a few Englishmen as well, including one, a man of the East Lancashire Regiment, who had been captured in 1914. He was obviously worn out and looked grey.

We slept in a big lodging house that had been used pre-war by Italian migrant workers. Wire had been put around the building and there was a guardhouse, the place being known as Kommando 19. Bunks had been built and there were mattresses and blankets, so we couldn't grumble about the conditions there. The factory itself was quite large and relied on many hundreds of tons of limestone rock dug from the mines and transported down the river Rhine. We would be taken by the factory train down to the harbour, where two men would climb down a ladder into the hold of a barge, one to each corner, pick up a hammer and get cracking – literally! It was important to try and find the grain to break the rock open with one bang as it saved a lot of strength. Then to preserve our hands, we would use a fork to load these coconut-sized pieces into a hopper lowered on a chain into the barge. When it was full, the crane lifted the hopper out of the barge and the contents were emptied into a truck and taken by private railway about two miles to the factory. There it was mixed with some coke and put down a chimney and burnt. What was left was mixed with a liquid chemical, the outcome of which was soda used in making concrete for buildings at home or making pill boxes or dugouts at the front.

We were woken by the guards at four o'clock in the morning and started work at just after six o'clock, until six at night. We were under constant supervision all day, guards walking up and down on the harbour wall, their rifles slung over their shoulders. They tended not to bother us too much because they knew if we didn't work hard to fill our quota, then at lunch time we would have to stay down there. We would have approximately two hours off during the day, half-an-hour at 8am, an hour for lunch at 12 noon and another half-an-hour at 4pm, so it was ten hours' actual work, which was a long day and six days a week too. The point is this, it was tough, I mean this was the kind of work that I was not used to. I'd always been a pen pusher, always in an office of some kind since leaving school at fourteen to work in a bank. Coming suddenly to breaking up rock or unloading a truck filled with coal was something new to me and very hard. The rock came in blocks often about the length of a door and you had to use a very heavy hammer and cut that down into smaller pieces. Well, you'd know you'd got something on your hands – probably blisters – and, if we didn't do it, then we didn't get our bowl of soup.

I did other work, too. One was unloading slack coal, that is, coal that had been through a screen to bring it to a certain size, in our case about an inch square, so that it would burn quicker. Each truck held twenty tons of coal and it would be the job of two men to unload two trucks a day. We could not just open the truck door and let the coal fall out, no, all the coal had to be thrown by a shovel on to a high pile that was some distance away and required some effort. On one or two occasions, when the guards were not in my vicinity, I did deliberately open the side door and let some coal out onto the track to cause trouble. That was my duty, to interfere with the German war effort if I could. If a train started to pull out, the truck would go off the rails and of course if it happened to be a truck that I'd been working on they'd be after 121, shouting out my POW number. I would stand and look at them – me – look as innocent as any Englishman could. On other -occasions I would just go and hide, deliberately go into a corner, squat down in a truck and shut my eyes and wait for the Germans to yell out my number. Obviously they'd create such a row the other sentries would come up to look, at which point I would appear looking as innocent as a baby. They'd shout at me and I'd just shrug my shoulders, as if I didn't understand.

JACK ROGERS

In a corner of this camp there were latrines for all the prisoners, and with all the men and the different nations having nothing but mangel wurzel water and bread, they were all on the run. So of course it's a continual parade of men going up and down to the latrine, backwards and forwards all day if they weren't working.

My first job was on what they called the sanitary police. Behind the camp latrines were troughs, well, everything that was dropped, all the sewage, went into these trenches, covered over by two big doors. My job, along with five others, was to go to the trenches with a great big barrel on four wheels. Two of us would open these troughs, one each, and we used to have a big long piece of wood, like a big oar, with which to keep stirring up the sewage until you made it into a very fine liquid. The third member of the party would lower a bucket on a chain into the sewage and pull it up and hand it to a man standing on a ladder alongside the barrel. He'd take it up and empty his bucket until the barrel was practically filled. When it was full, we took the muck to the allotment, a small strip of land which ran right the way round the outside of the camp. There was a great big tap on the barrel and from it we filled up our buckets, which we emptied over the ground, spreading it out. My gosh, the stench, on a windy day when the wind was blowing into the camp, it was awful. The Germans were growing these mangel wurzels, their main crop other than potatoes. They seemed to like them somehow and the result was, when they did grow, they grew to two feet high or more, and the Germans practically lived on those at the cookhouse or took them home to their families. We didn't get any, not to my knowledge. All we got was the juice that they used to cook those things in, the 'gravy' we called it. It was a thickish water with bits floating in it and you were lucky if you got a few in your tin, something to chew on.

TOMMY GAY

I was soon transferred to a camp close to a mine pithead, where the railway trucks picked up the coal. We lived in huts with barbed wire all the way round and sentries, although the camp was part of the mine itself. There were four mines in the area called Denenbaum, the biggest being the Prinzregent, one of the largest in Germany. You could be picked to go to any of these mines but I was mostly in one called Julius Philipp along with several hundred Russians, Frenchmen, Portuguese and Englishmen. There were two mine collapses there and two or three men were killed, although I didn't see them as they either took place in a different part of the mine or on a different shift.

I worked with a German as no two Englishmen went down the mine together, just in case we blew it up. It depended on the person you worked with as to how much you did. The shifts were 6am to 2pm, 2pm to 10pm, 10pm until 6am, eight hour shifts, and you took it in turns to rotate around the clock. I was frightened, I wondered what on earth had happened when one second I was in light and the next I was in the blackest blackness, because the cage went so fast it took my breath. I thought, 'Oh God, that's it' but no, I was down the bottom of the mine and then there's air and water, there's always a little river of water alongside the track and then you pass the stables where the pit ponies go, and the stables are all whitewashed. There are fire doors every hundred yards or so that must be shut behind you and there's a rush of wind along the shaft – marvellous, I thought how clever it is down under the earth like this.

I was sent to the end of the seam. The German would pick

away at the seam of coal and all I did was shovel it up into another truck until it was full. Then I'd push the truck to the end of the line where a lift took it up and away, and an empty truck would come down. You could see the seam shining against the ordinary earth. I don't remember any targets, I worked according to the German I was with, but whoever it was, it was work all day, work all day. Sometimes you would get a miserable civilian to work with and he would tell you – in German of course – 'We want as many trucks as we can get, zwanzig trucks, twenty trucks if we can'. Twenty trucks was a lot of coal, yes, yes, twenty trucks was a lot of coal. And naturally I'd have a good old swear at him, he didn't know, and I'd think to myself, 'Yeah, you'll be lucky, you'll get what I can do, that's all.' If he said it properly then I would do what I could, but if he was nasty with his talk, Tom didn't do as he wanted.

FRANK DEANE

Afterwards, I was transferred into the general barracks for about a month or so and then out on Kommando. We went to Minden and then walked to a little village where there was a barrel factory on the river Weser. Part of the factory, probably the headquarters, was in Minden and part was on the river-bank in a village called Wacker, about 10km away from Minden. I never saw a whole barrel, I think they must have made them in stages. They'd cut the wood somewhere, shape them elsewhere and steam and bend them in the machine room. We were billeted in a half-finished house with no doors or windows. In various other places round about the factory and in the barracks there were French, Russians, Poles and Italians. Food was the worst until we got Red Cross parcels. We never had a bath or anything of that sort for a long time. On Kommando we'd got some enamel pots and pans and we used to have a wood-burning stove and we'd boil up water in these pots and pans and tip the water into a bucket, take it up into the attic and have a wash all over. That would be about four months after I was captured and until then I'd never had a bath or a shave or anything of that sort for a long, long time.

The Germans were quite amiable, and we were quite amiable with them, in fact we used to tease them quite a bit, although they never quite understood whether to take it seriously or not. The Germans had a lot of timber cut up into lengths and piled into large stacks to put out to season, and one of our jobs was to knock these down and load them onto trolleys and wheel them into the machine shops. We could sometimes idle about and do nothing and the women would come out of the machine shop with the -trolleys, and wonder why we had not been in, as they were being held up with their work. We also had to unload logs off barges, and on another -occasion we unloaded a lorry full of bricks. We didn't want to help the Germans any more than we could, so in a sense it was a duty as well as a pleasure to do as much shirking as possible.

NORMAN COWAN

Norman's blinded friend, Billy Watson, was sent on the same train journey to Quedlinburg. Billy's sight had not recovered at all since he had been struck by shrapnel in the same attack in which Norman had been wounded.

I was to become Billy Watson's guide and eyes, as he remained blind. It became my duty, although I was rather crippled, to guide and help him in his great disability and he became very dependent on me. The one advantage was that he could eat three bowls of soup because he couldn't see it. It looked awful. He'd say, 'Norman, are you eating your soup?' And I'd say, 'No, do you want it?' And he would.

I had been instructed by the doctor and the committee to

guide Billy about the British compound, so I was not at the time called to do outside duties such as working in the salt mines or brick kilns. Later, I was told to report with Billy each week to the German medical staff, who were interested in what progress Billy's sight might have made. In the end, the doctors decided not to operate again and sadly for myself but happily for him, in late October 1918 he was repatriated to a London hospital for further tests and an operation.

Quite early after our arrival, we were ordered to parade in the compound to be checked for vermin. Two pairs of horse-clipping shears manned by German soldiers were brought and all our hair on our scalps and bodies was cut off. At this time I couldn't walk properly and had developed an almost permanent limp. Still weakened but improving, I was put on a light bogie which ran on a single line railway into the carrot and turnip fields. It was frosty then and if you couldn't dig the carrots up, you got no carrots. I was still very crippled with the deep wound but managed with the aid of a stick to hobble along and do my turn in the carrot fields for the compound's soup. I was immensely grateful to a British doctor and two Red Cross assistants for the daily attention to my wound which, with their constant efforts and dressings, eventually cleared of pus and started to heal.

Eventually I got better enough and I was sent to the salt mines, which I had dreaded. They supplied us with light blue canvas trousers, cardboard peaked hats, wooden shovels and wooden sabots, my boots having been taken away or stolen. I was walking with a stick and I now joined the shufflers who swore and walked along to the light railway where the open bogies took us some considerable distance, choo-choo-chooing into a drift mine. We would put our lights on and see the pillars of salt half as high as a house, being dug by ex-perienced miners. The man in charge of all the POWs turned out to be a friend of mine, Sergeant Tommy Paterson from Chopwell, whom I'd known when I was training at Tidworth. He'd been a miner all his life until he'd enlisted and been captured on the Somme in 1916. He knew how to leave certain pillars of salt and how to use wood to shore up the roof.

Near the entrance of this mine was a great pile of salt, quite dirty, and for POWs who were not fully fit, even shovelling the salt into the bogies was very arduous. Occasionally a bogie would come off the rails and there was a great cheer from the British soldiers, but there wasn't a cheer when they were told to put it back. Very soon, many were unable to continue and fell into sickness or deep fatigue. I wasn't used to shovelling and I got a bet hand, a miners' complaint caused by shovel-handle friction on the palm of the hand which caused an abscess in the muscles. When I was in Britain as a boy, sixteen years and three months old, I was licking stamps for an office. I wasn't fit. I'd been badly wounded and you don't get wounded and simply come back to full strength, do you? At least I don't. It was very, very tiring and you got exhausted because you didn't have the wherewithal to support you. If you'd had beef and port and chicken, we would have been able to do it, but I couldn't and had to be sent back to camp.

BILL EASTON

I was thin, they told me I looked like a skeleton, ragged. But I tried not to worry. You see, a lot of men, I swear, died just of worry and anxiety. They used to say, 'Young Bill, he doesn't trouble,' they thought I didn't care, but I did. There was no point being miserable and I'll admit I didn't expect to last out the war, but I used to say, 'well, what's the use in worrying?'

We were digging roads or artesian wells, sinking a pipe down until we touched water. I used to collapse and of course if you collapsed they'd give you a thump and pull you to one side and throw water over you until you came round. I wasn't right. I was delirious sometimes, so I don't remember a lot about it. I do recall we went out on road-mending one time and I was just about passing out. I couldn't lift the pickaxe up so I said to the fellow next to me, 'I shan't be able to stick this out much longer, I shall collapse.' I really thought I would die there. Out of the camp, when there were perhaps just eight or nine of you, that's where I found the guards knocked you about most, give you a proper clout so you end up on your knees and couldn't get up. This man, he told me it was a pity I hadn't got a trade. I said, 'What do you mean?' And he said, 'If you were a carpenter or something like that.' So I said, 'I'm not a carpenter but I'm an upholsterer.' He told me several of the lads were working in the village on different jobs that weren't too bad and that I should put my name down. So I did. I was what the Germans called a Sattler.

A group of five of us went to this village, and as we passed this hotel the guard told me to wait there. A girl came out, friendly looking, and I told her I was a Sattler. She told me to follow her and I was taken into the hotel ballroom which had no floor. At one end of the room was a stack of floorboards. She didn't speak English and she said something to me that I didn't understand and she went out and the door banged shut. So I thought to myself, 'What do I have to do?' Although I was an upholsterer, my father had been a carpenter for a while and during the school holidays he had refused to let me lounge about and had taught me about working with wood. All the wood had been cut to length and there was every type of saw, plane and hammer, so I decided I couldn't sit there all day and began to lay this floor and got quite into it.

This lady was Leni Mörrs and she lived at the hotel and quickly made a right fuss of me. There was no one staying at the hotel except the owner, an old lady, and some of her family. I found out that while she couldn't speak English, she could understand a bit and between us we got on famously. She used to bring me cups of coffee and cigarettes – although I didn't smoke – and if there were any odd jobs around the village, particularly if they were to do with chairs or sofas, like a broken spring, she would take me round and I would fix them. This was now towards the end of the war and the guards of Friedrichsfeld camp were becoming very slipshod. They were supposed to come and collect me every night, but it got to the point when Leni used to walk me back to the camp. Everybody knew her. At the camp, you walked through the gates and into a sort of funnel. The British boys used to shout out all sorts of things: 'What! Are you bringing your wife home with you this time?' and 'Cor, I bet she's nice and warm at night.' I told them to pipe down as Leni would have a fit if she knew what they were saying. They told me later that she did know, that one of the guards was translating what they'd said to her. And do you know, she never turned a hair.

She used to say, 'Kommen Sie mit' and off we'd go to do various jobs. One Saturday, instead of going into the village, she took me across the railway tracks and then off into a field. I asked where we were going and she said, 'Wesel'. We went over more fields and then came to a canal. We walked along the bank until we came in sight of the village and then we shot off and went down a lane. Nobody could see us. We kept to tiny alleys before we came to a house and went in. There was a lady there and I was given tea, only the tea was British tea and the milk was Nestlé milk. It was beautiful. She put her finger up to say, 'Don't speak, keep quiet.' A sandbag was brought full of little tins, after which we left the house and walked miles round back to Friedrichsfeld village. Back at the hotel, we went into the kitchen and Leni locked all the doors. There was a big cupboard and she opened it and there was no end of food in there. After a time, a German officer came and knocked on the door. He spoke to Leni and out came the key, the cupboard was unlocked and he took some food and cleared off. I didn't see any money being exchanged so I don't know what the deal was, but this was all smuggled food. The house in Wesel was only a couple of miles from Holland and food was being brought there before being sent on, ending up in places like the hotel.

JACK ROGERS

Now and again, we'd be called out on parade and a party of men would be formed, then sent away to go down the mines. It would be made up of different nationalities; I don't know who used to choose, but names would be read out and these men would be responsible for getting themselves prepared to leave on the Monday. Many of the poor chaps who had been down the mine would be brought up and taken into hospital. They were used as slave labour, as we called it, so they were calling out the names and numbers of the new lot that they'd picked to go down the mines in their places. Well, mine was amongst them and of course I didn't know what to do, I didn't like the thought of that at all. I didn't know where in Germany it would be, whether it would be a coal mine, a lead mine, tin mine, or salt mine. The following Sunday, we'd got this entertainment show in the barracks coming off so I said to the sergeant major, I said, 'Look, they got me down to go to the mines on Monday and we're doing this show, we're getting it all together.' He said, 'Leave it to me, Jack, I'll go and see what I can do.' So he went and saw the interpreter and in the end they found a bloke that had been a miner and he said he didn't mind going, so his name was put on the list and mine taken off. While in the trenches, I had been buried alive by a shell that had landed on the parapet. I was dug out and was lucky to survive, but even to this day I don't like to be enclosed too tightly anywhere. That incident left an impression on me all my life.

The Germans had found out that my previous trade in civvie life was as a shoemaker. In the camp, there was a wood shoe shop and they employed a good many prisoners working in teams of two, making wooden shoes all day long. I used to go and collect my food ration in the morning, a can of tea and a piece of bread and go to this shop where they gave me a Frenchman to work with whose name happened to be similar to mine, Roget, his name was. We used to stand at a

93

double bench and get these great big chunks of wood and it was my job to saw them up into given widths and lengths. Then I'd pass them over to Roget and he'd put them in a vice and then use a mechanical scoop to bore a hole into the wood big enough for a foot to go into. He then shaped the sides of the shoe and then handed them back for me to trim round the sides.

Occasionally we were taken as a party down to the railway station, where a small hand crane was used to shift the logs of wood onto a cart, two men pulling and two pushing the cart back to the camp. One of the guards was a decent chap and he used to take us round some of the back streets and into the back garden of a little local pub, where he treated us to a lager. Well, in our Red Cross packages there used to be bars of toilet soap and they were absolutely worth a fortune in Germany. One of us used to give this German a bar of soap, and that did the trick. He was so pleased to be able to take home a bar of scented soap to his wife that from then on he was willing to pay for eight or more of us to have a lager.

PERCY WILLIAMS

In early September, I was sent up to Güstrow POW camp in Mecklenburg, then soon afterwards I went by cattle truck to work at the shipyards at Bremerhaven, at a place called Geestemünde at the mouth of the Weser. I was what was known as a catcherboy. Red-hot rivets were thrown up to the side of the ship, and my job was to get hold of these rivets with tongs and take them to be bolted down before they cooled, helping to fix the plates on the side of the ship. You had to be careful, these rivets were thrown up in twos and threes and landed on the floor, and it was important not to tread on one. I often had to jump out of the road to avoid them. Mind, you were under their thumb so there was no complaining, you had to damn well do as you were told.

ERNIE STEVENS

Ernie had endured breaking up rock at the harbour, which was desperately hard work. However, his fortunes were to change for the better when he met Friedrich Rosen.

The factory was a big building, hundreds worked there, turning out tons and tons of soda powder every day. One of the workers there was Friedrich Rosen, a German with whom I was very friendly. We had to stir up the liquid and the soda powder with steel rakes so that it flowed through the channel and wouldn't settle at the bottom as it passed by us. Now there were only three of us in that department. There was the foreman, who slept most of the night, and there was Friedrich and myself. He had never been in the army because as a young man he had been shot in an eye with an air gun and was not able to see. There was no slacking except when he was about. He was very decent to me and treated me humanely. On one occasion, I asked if he would like a tin of bully beef that I'd received in my Red Cross packet, if he'd bring me potatoes. I knew he grew potatoes and he said, 'I'll bring you potatoes every day', and he did, too. So we were able to have baked potatoes and fried potatoes and all kinds of potatoes, and it added to our diet and gave us a good meal.

When we were on the night shift, he occasionally used to go and have a sleep whilst I looked after things and made sure we were not surprised by the bosses, and then he would allow me to go and have a sleep. So he was a good pal. I'd made it my business to upset the Germans when I could, but that did not extend to Freddie because he looked after my interests. I made a distinction between those who were rotten and those who were trying to be friendly, even if that friendship was guarded.

In the room where I slept, there was a stove which stood over a fire. There was always plenty of coal that could be brought from the factory to fuel the fire. At the top of the stove, men had put wire and fastened it, and hanging on that wire were tins of water, so they could make the tea or coffee that came in their parcels. We could also write cards or letters, which we were allowed to send every tenth day, but we could not mention the war. Do not mention what you thought of Germans, do not castigate them, do not give them a bad name. To receive a letter, well, it was great to hear from my mother and to know people at home were doing well as far as possible. She never mentioned the war, she never mentioned air raids, she kept away from anything to do with the war. She just wrote about their own health and how they were, which was important, and I used to think every minute of the day about my mum and my little half sister.

JACK ROGERS

Relief from the daily grind of camp life came in the form of concerts, staged for the entertainment of the prisoners, by the prisoners themselves. Everything from sing-songs to opera, from light skits to full-blown plays, were rehearsed and performed, with sets and costumes that would have put many a repertory theatre to shame. Jack Rogers was an eager participant.

The French and some of the Italians used to put on concerts in one of the big extended huts that the prisoners had been allowed to build. They had made a little theatre with a stage, and brought in chairs of some sort for seats. There were plays there and on one occasion I sang there with a friend called Mac. I have a picture taken by a Frenchman of me holding Mac's hand. I remember we were performing and he said, 'Wait, hold it' and he took the picture. I think we were singing the song, 'If you were the only girl in the world and I was the only boy'. That was one little turn we did there. Mac had borrowed a sort of dress suit and I had a frock somebody lent me. Various shows were being put on every fortnight in the camp, but I asked our sergeant major if he could get permission to put on a little concert ourselves, which he did. So about once a month we put on a concert, rehearsing in our hut at night to find out what talent we'd got. But we never had a great lot of talent, I can assure you of that. The concerts were full, as many as they could get in, they'd all come.

I was talking with Roget and I asked him if the French would let me do a turn at one of their big concerts. I told him I had done quite a bit of entertaining at the front with the 59th Divisional Concert Party, called 'The Crumps'. I'd sing, tell a few jokes and did impersonations of different people like George Robey and Harry Champion. So Roget said he would arrange it with the fellow producing the French concert, a funny man, a comedian, and he called himself 'Tonic Sol Fa'. The Germans always occupied the front three rows at these shows, then the French and if there were any room left, a few of the British could come in, so I'd been able to see what they had done before. I told them I could do a bit of a song and that an Italian I knew would play the music. I decided I was going to do a monologue called 'Spotty'. Then I would sing a song called 'Henry the Eighth I am', as well as a song from Sam Mayo called 'A One Man Band'.

They liked the songs, but one the soldiers always enjoyed was 'Spotty' a monologue about when we'd been soldiers. I'll shorten it a bit but it went something like:

> Now Spotty was my chum he was a ginger headed bloke
> An everlasting gas bag and as stubborn as a moke
> He gave us all the 'ump he did before it came to war
> By sporting all his bits of French what no one asked him for
> He said to me "old son", he said "you won't stand half a chance
> When I gets in conversation with the demoiselles of France."

We had days of hell together till they told us to retire

And then Spotty's flow of language set the water carts
on fire

But him and me was very lucky for two thirds of us
was dead

With the gleaming black marias and the shrapnel
overhead

And every time they missed us when the fire was
murderous hot

Old Spotty says 'encore, encore', that's French for
rotten shot.

And then at last there came a time we'd got 'em on
the go

And him and me was fighting at a little place called
Mo

We was lying down together in a hole dug with our
hands

For you gets it quick and sudden if you moves about
or stands

We was sharing half a fag we was, yes, turn and turn
about

When I felt him crawl towards me and he said, "Oh
mate, I'm Out."

And his eyes they couldn't see me, they never will no
more

With his twisted mouth he whispered "So long mate
au revoir"

There was no one quite the same to me for him and
me was pals

And if I could only have him with me you could keep
your fancy girls

But whatever place he's gone to I don't ask nothing
more

Than to line up with him like that, so long, Spotty, au
revoir.

Was it important to keep up camp morale? Rather, if you could. The Germans used to come and sit there, even the German officers in the front. They used not to understand much, I might tell you, but of course we were always pretty good at knowing when someone had had a little dig at the Germans and we would cheer and clap. Even in our barrack huts on a Sunday night, we could get anybody who could recite something or perhaps tell a funny story. We called it our Barrack Room Gaffe and men would sing and everybody would join in the choruses. So we managed to make some sort of entertainment. It helped to pass the time as the men were getting pretty down at one time. When the food was coming through and we had a bit of tobacco, then the men became much better company. We were forever thinking that the war wouldn't last, that we should get home, so it was no good giving in completely. We just had to try and keep going, keep ourselves fit, our spirits up.

TOMMY GAY

We tried to form a band. One of the French members was a musician and a member of the band and was teaching some of us how to play different instruments. I managed to buy a clarinet with the money we earned and other people brought a drum and so on. We played after a style but we weren't musicians. We played on a Sunday when we had our day off and we had no work to do, it made life a little bit more cheerful because it took our mind off our hunger. I mean, it was such a lovely change to have something that would make us smile and laugh instead of the war all the time.

JACK ROGERS

For Jack, as for many soldiers, camp entertainment was a welcome distraction from reality. Life was never easy, not for anyone, but it could be made much worse if prisoners had to contend with a vindictive commandant or a brutal guard.

During the war, the British and the Germans had come to an agreement to exchange prisoners who had been badly wounded and could not fight again. The commandant at our camp was one of these, a tall man who had been partially blinded and wore black glasses. He hated the British like poison, and never missed a chance to vent his spite on us. For example, the British were noted for trying to keep their huts fairly clean, whereas the Russians had a reputation of being some of the dirtiest people in the camp, using the corner of their huts as toilets instead of going to the latrines. So every now and again, perhaps once a month, this German would parade everybody on a Saturday and swapped us all round, and we were always made to change with the Russians, so we had to occupy their dirty hut and they went to our clean one. I tell you, we never forgave him for that. Then on a Sunday morning, our one day off, he would get us out in the pouring rain, just the British, mind you, and he would make us march round and round and round the camp until he was fed up himself.

The commandant called us schweinehunde, he never addressed us in any other way. Through his interpreter he'd start to talk to you, 'Schweine-hunde' and then he gave you the message. He used to have his spite on us every now and again, having us march round and round the square for an hour or so. On one occasion it was raining and he was standing there watching, puffing away at what looked like a small cheroot, a little cigar. He was standing with his back to our hut windowsill where presumably he must have put it down when he went over to talk to the interpreter. Of course we're marching round and someone couldn't resist the temptation to pick the cigar up, so that when the commandant went back it was gone and he began looking all round on the ground. Of course, nobody was going to own up that they'd pinched it, so he kept us there. All he did say was we'd got to march on and keep marching until somebody found it and brought it back and that's what he kept us doing nearly all day Sunday, just because he'd lost the end of his cigar. We were already weak, no strength, so you can imagine how we felt, soaking wet. We'd all had to suffer – that was the sort of man he was. Finally, they had to send us off indoors and we were completely worn out by this bloody man.

There were times when some of the prisoners couldn't help but lose their tempers and started to fight, well, they'd be punished immediately. Similarly, if you were out on working parties and weren't working hard enough, the Germans would think nothing about hitting you with a shovel, you know what I mean, there were no other means of immediate punishment and there were no rules laid down. The men down the mines suffered most, because the Germans were paid by the truck load and if prisoners weren't working hard enough, the Germans would give them a smash with a shovel, knock 'em about. Quite a number of our chaps were injured like that and came back into the hospital. They'd tell you while they walked round the hospital yard recovering, they'd come up and tell you through the wire. Once or twice we had chaps who'd try and escape. They'd got away somewhere and been captured and brought back and they were put in the prison yard and they were in pretty bad shape sometimes.

TOMMY GAY

We were coming back from work one time and we saw a German officer walking by and we got the order from the sentry 'Augen links', which means 'eyes left' and somebody blew a raspberry. That German went nearly mad. He drew his sword out and had a good mind to swipe someone with it. It was a good job he couldn't tell who'd done it. He was shouting in German but of course we couldn't understand a word and the chap who'd done it, well, no man's going to admit to it, of course not, because we know bloody well he's in for a good hiding.

When someone did wrong, then collectively we would all have to go and stand by the wire fencing to attention and they called it 'Stillstand'. And if they saw you move, if you tried to rest one leg by leaning on the other, they would come and bump their rifles up against you, 'Come on Engländer, come on Engländer', make you stand straight. Naturally, as soon as he went, perhaps to the next man, you'd rest the other leg for a second, just for a fraction of time, and then he'd come back again and do the same thing again, bump the other leg with the butt, just to remind you that you were being punished. The threat was there to make it worse, make you stand there even longer, make you do it, but then you'd drop down, you couldn't do it.

Perhaps we weren't working fast enough, shovelling up the coal that was being cut out of the seam. Not working hard enough, that was the main reason for punishment, down there underground. There would be occasional rows down below and the German would report you when you came up, you had to slog hard all the time.

BILL EASTON

In the camp, the guards had something like a metronome and a voice, the camp interpreter I should think, was saying to us, 'Come on, you so and sos, you're still British soldiers. We know you're good at marching, let's see you step out.' Some of us could barely lift our feet but this metronome kept on, click, click, click as we went round the ground. Guards could be brutal. One or two would take it out on you if they got you on your own. Some would hit you just as a matter of habit, on a march if you straggled a bit, they'd go along hitting you into position. Others, if they thought you were dodging work, would give you a clout, in the end you got hardened to it. Anyone who's been hit in the back, the lower part of your back, you'd feel that for days, let alone anything else, because those rifles, they were shod with brass, heavy brass and you'd feel as if the rifle was going right through you. Right in the kidneys, just at your hips. At first you are stunned but after about half an hour you're as stiff as a board and awake all night. In the morning, your back would be a damn sight worse but you were still expected to go and work. But I've seen chaps and they couldn't get up and if they did they simply collapsed. If you were out on a working party, they really bullied you, you didn't get a minute, particularly if you were isolated with a fellow and he didn't like the job. If you were mending the road, you had to stop sometimes and then if they saw you straightening up they'd come up behind you and bang! I'll admit I didn't get a lot of it, but some of the lads, if they turned round and swore, they were set upon by two or three guards. By the time they'd finished, some of his mates had to come and help him back to the camp and into hospital. It was a wonder some of those guards weren't murdered, but we couldn't do anything.

TOMMY GAY

Medical treatment was rough and generally rudimentary. For those in the mines, like Tommy Gay, visiting the doctor might be the only way to survive, even if it meant self-mutilation.

The doctor at the mine was hard. I remember one man with boils all down his arm and the doctor just squashed them, bust them open, shocking, what a wicked thing to do, unnaturally brutal.

Some men would injure themselves. Talking to some of your mates in your camp, on your bunk, some would say that they were going sick tomorrow. 'I'm going to put a couple of fingers in front of the truck tomorrow, split them, make them bleed.' It got them out of the mine, they'd have to report sick and have it looked at by the doctor. And they would put their hand in front of two trucks and pinch their fingers and split them, make them bleed, and they'd have to go to the doctor, report sick. But at times you thought you might as well shoot yourself, best out of the way, because who wanted to live, working and starving hungry? And that feeling came across me many times, 'come and blow us to pieces'.

FREDERICK HAMMOND

One day, I got a letter from my mother saying that a mate of mine, a bank clerk, Percy Dawes, was missing and his parents hadn't heard anything of him at all. He wasn't in my battalion but that very same day he came into the camp and was put into the next bed to me. He'd been working down a salt mine and I understood him to say that he'd deliberately crushed his fingers to get out, he was so desperate and so weak. He was just like a skeleton, dreadful. The men in the barracks would be up to all sorts of tricks to get out of work, sometimes they would bandage their hands up so tight at night that they'd swell up. The men on the ward clubbed together and we helped him out with our parcels. I was for exchange and I left him lying in the camp, and that was the last I heard, until his parents told my parents that we'd saved his life.

CHAPTER FIVE

The Agony of Hunger

For British soldiers forced to rely on German food, there was no alternative to living in an almost permanent state of hunger. Hunger preyed on the mind and played havoc with digestion systems. Hunger wore prisoners down physically and mentally and could turn friends into enemies. Of all the torments about which prisoners unanimously complained, it was the lack of food, day in, day out, that was both the most insidious and the most demoralising.

Like many other aspects of POW life, there were rules governing what a prisoner could expect to receive. International agreements that nations should supply their prisoners with foodstuffs roughly equal to those received by troops at the front were agreed, but in reality they were simply a pipe dream. It never happened. For the British soldiers captured early in the war, the treatment they received and the quality and quantity of food they were given, was affected by the attitude the Germans had to British soldiers.

Unlike the conscript armies of France and Russia, the British army was professional, and as such its soldiers were considered to be little more than mercenaries. Even worse were the men of Kitchener's army, for they had willingly enlisted to fight the Kaiser and were beneath contempt. One wounded prisoner recalled later that as he lay on the operating table he was asked what type of soldier he was. He replied that he was a regular, whereupon he was told that the surgeon would not have operated had he been a volunteer. Later on in the war, it was the Allied naval blockade of German ports for which soldiers were generally blamed. The worsening con-ditions in Germany, they were told, were due to the activities of the Royal Navy, which acted as a principal enforcer. If the Germans could barely feed their own troops at the front, if people were starving to death in the countryside, then what right had the prisoners to expect food?

No matter where men were, food meant little more than starvation rations. Typically, each man would receive a mug of ersatz coffee made from burnt barley or acorns, and a thin slice of black bread, adulterated with sawdust. At lunch he might have soup of varying quality, but generally it was little more than the water in which guards had boiled their own meals, with odd pieces of vegetable floating around. For those working close to the lines in France, eating grass was often the only source of immediate grati-fication while grabbing the leaves of nettles or cale offered the hope of boiling them up later, perhaps with a few potato peelings. Many men in their desperation to fill the void in their stomachs drank copiously, but this was dangerous and, combined with their semi-liquid diet of thin soup and bread, caused many men to suffer terrible stomach problems. The result was dropsy, a poten-tially fatal illness caused by the consumption of too much liquid as opposed to solids.

In camps, the food was prepared by prisoners lucky enough to get a job in the cookhouse. Here, large vats were used to heat up the food which was then distributed in caul-drons, buckets or dixies to the men. Queues were formed, with one man ladling the food into the prisoner's mess tin, whereupon he would either eat the food there and then or take it back to his hut. Sometimes a loaf of bread would be issued to six men or more, one of whom would be chosen to divide up the valuable food. To ensure that no one received more or less than they deserved and to avoid arguments, primitive weighing scales were made.

For men on working parties, the issuing of food provided a further torment. Often supplied with food for a twenty-four, even a forty-eight, hour period, men were forced to make an agonising decision. They could eat it all straight away for temporary relief, knowing no further food would be given, or they could eke out what little they had throughout the day, realising that the hunger pains would only lessen but never cease. Many chose the former, knowing full well they would regret the decision later, but being unable to look at food without eating it. For those chosen for hard physical labour, the decision when to eat or not could make the difference between surviving the day intact, being punished, or even ending up in hospital.

It might seem surprising that, given the nature of their plight, prisoners often chose to think, daydream or talk about their hunger. Often, as they lay on their bunks, men described their favourite recipes and what they would eat when they got back to Britain. It was as if the problem of hunger, once shared, was halved and not doubled as one might expect, as if the memory of some home-made dish was nevertheless comforting while agonising at the same time. As men's letters were subject to strict censorship, few could tell relatives at home of how close to starving they really were. One prisoner did sent word on his eventual release that his family should disregard everything he'd ever written in his letters home about having adequate food, but it was possibly only the men from such places as the Isle of Lewis who could send coded word of their true plight. In their letters home they all spoke of a Mr Acres; Mr Acres in Gaelic was Mr Hungry.

The obsession with food led to pilfering, not just from the Germans, but from each other. Hunger was a great leveller. Similarly, on rare occasions when food, however rancid, was abandoned, men could end up fighting over the scraps, pushing each other out of the way. It disgusted some who watched. Bartering with the Germans was one alternative source of extra food, but for those with little or nothing to swap or sell, stealing was the only way. Working in the cook-house, or in the fields, offered men the chance to take a little extra and many men went to great lengths to secrete a potato or hide an onion which could be eaten later. If they were caught, the punishment varied, depending on the camp, but many were willing to take the chance. It wasn't until men were placed on a list for regimental, or, later, Red Cross parcels that conditions improved. Even then, there were those who, for one reason or another, were never registered, and for them it was only death or an Armistice that would release them from their interminable hunger.

GEORGE GADSBY

Amongst the most hungry of all prisoners were those, like George Gadsby, who had been kept in France. Often beyond the reach of any food aid, many survived only on what the enemy deigned to give them, or what they could scrounge.

We began to feel the pinch of hunger and thirst, and we had marched some 16 miles before we got a drink, reaching the Somme Canal. At 4pm we arrived at another cage and were given a tenth of a loaf of black bread (the first since our capture), and after marching another 5 miles reached Caudry, 60 miles from the place of our capture. Here we received a little soup flavoured with preserved horseflesh, but nevertheless they kindly provided us with palliasses to lie on. As we approached Caudry, the civilians tried hard to give us a little bread but the Germans charged them from time to time with their lances and went within an inch of thrusting them into their bodies. One brave woman threw us half a loaf of bread from her bedroom window and the sentry put his lance through every pane.

We remained at Caudry for three days, receiving a quarter of a loaf of black bread and a bowl of thin soup each day. Many of our boys gave away valuable watches, cigarette cases and wallets for a small portion of black bread with which to ease their hunger a little.

We left Caudry on 29th March, after three miserable days confined in a factory, and proceeded to Le Quesnoy. We had to march a distance of 20 miles with a paltry halt of 10 minutes. Our sentries were, of course, on horseback.

We arrived at Le Quesnoy on the afternoon of Good Friday and were placed in a cage built in the centre of a field. After we'd marched that long distance of 30 kilometres, they greeted us with a bowl of barley water. As the evening approached, we began to realise what it was to be a prisoner in the hands of the Huns. We had no overcoat or jerkin and the night was so terribly cold that we were obliged to walk up and down that solitary area with the mud over our ankles. Occasionally, utterly exhausted, we would lie down for probably half an hour but this was all too long, as we had to walk about with renewed energy to regain our circulation.

On one side of the cage they had constructed a latrine by digging a trench and erecting poles across. Here many of our fellow prisoners sat and went to sleep, the ground being too damp and muddy to lie down upon.

On the Saturday night, rain poured in torrents and we stood at the gate herded together like a flock of sheep, asking the Germans now and again to find us some shelter, but still in this wretched condition they did not pity our plight. The Hun sergeant major replied with such answers as 'Tell Lloyd George to stop the war' and 'Your friends in the trenches have no shelter.'

At length we realised that asking for cover was in vain, and so, following the example of some new arrivals, we comforted ourselves a little, but not the Germans, with a good 'sing-song'.

The sentries during the day sold us cigarettes at four for a shilling (we brought similar cigarettes at 20 for a shilling afterwards from the French civilians at Cambrai). As at Caudry, we gave away any valuables or keepsakes we had for a little bread.

Sunday and Monday passed along and we began to feel

very weak, having little food, our rations only consisting of a quarter of a loaf of black bread and a bowl of soup as it was called, diluted 90% with water.

I, with two friends of my battalion, dug a hole in a heap of sand and, as we went to the cookhouse for our food, brought back each time a piece of wood with which we constructed a sufficient shelter to allow us to have a little sleep.

We had to bear this barbarity for six nights and seven days, confined to this barbed wire and muddy area. Several of our prisoners had to be taken out of the cage, overcome by exposure.

On the following Thursday, it rained continuously all day and in the evening the Germans placed us in a factory. Here we were packed together so tightly that it was impossible for anyone to lie down. We returned the next morning to the cage which we found in a very bad condition, rain having continued through the night.

On Friday afternoon, they marched us out of the cage and escorted us to some old houses. Here, although under cover, we had to sleep 26 to a room where there was only room for 10, whilst other men lay all over the staircase and in the old cellars. The place was in a filthy condition and the straw palliasses they gave us to lie on were covered with one mass of vermin. So numerous were these insects that, in the course of a day, our tunics and every garment were covered and it was impossible to sleep

Later in our captivity, we were supplied with an enamel bowl which we had to use for washing our clothes in and also as a container for our soup, if such it could be called. It usually consisted of sauerkraut very much diluted with water and flavoured with some portion of a beast usually given to cats. We very rarely got meat, and when we did manage to get a little, it consisted of horseflesh. We had one loaf of black bread between three of us, which had to last a day.

One or two sentries were very good and allowed the French people to give us food. One, I recall, told us to pick up our tools and marched us to a very big house, where he took us to the door and beckoned us in. Here, the lady of the house was awaiting us with a very good dinner. However, the remainder were down on us and would not allow us to receive anything.

Our minds were constantly troubled by the thought of hunger and we found it exceedingly hard to keep our thoughts from running into this groove. It was very rarely one went to bed without hearing someone say what he would like for supper, or listening to a description of the variety of foodstuffs which private 'so and so' had had on 'such and such' an occasion. I have often collected nettles from the roadside, and after being victorious in a scrimmage around the cookhouse for potato peelings, have boiled them together and prepared our supper. On another occasion, the German cook put a bowl of soup outside the cookhouse for his dog. The dog took a sniff and walked away from it. However, he did not get a second chance, as one of our prisoners put the soup into his mess tin and demolished the contents with relish.

WALTER HUMPHRYS

We lined up in fours, fives or sixes, depending on the size of the ration, and a German handed the outside man a loaf and he'd cut it into pieces. There were some quarrels over that sometimes, so we'd toss up occasionally if one piece was bigger than another. We might have had a smear of jam on our hand or a bit of grease, but that was it, one lick and it was gone. With that, we would probably have a bowl of sauerkraut or some ersatz coffee. We were always hungry. We used to pick a few mushrooms and mangolds as we cleared the old battlefields. It was repugnant eating mangolds, potato peelings, nettles and dandelions, but hunger finally overcame discretion. We became so weak that our legs shook under us, and a march of a mile or a mile and a half fatigued us. It took a long time before Red Cross parcels came. Towards the end of our time as prisoners, we came across labels from some of our parcels in a farmyard, obviously left by other prisoners who'd had parcels or ones which had been rifled, but we never got any ourselves, although one was returned to England when I got home.

THOMAS SPRIGGS

In the spring of 1918, they moved us to Tournai where we stayed a couple of days. I saw four Merseyside men fighting over a bucket of swill there, and that's all it was, pig swill. It had come from the kitchens, and it disgusted me to see them fighting over it, literally pushing each other away from the bucket before it toppled over and they had to scoop it up. I thought, 'Not me, I'd prefer to go hungry, I'd die rather than do anything like that.' An empty stomach, you drink loads and loads of water, I drank lots just to ease my stomach a bit. I felt really empty at times, really empty, but the Germans hadn't the food to give us.

I remember unloading some barbed wire one day from a truck, somewhere outside Valenciennnes. I scratched my wrists and they festered. I carried on for some weeks, but they wouldn't heal up properly, and yet as soon as we got our Red Cross parcels and I could get plenty of fat stuff down me, they healed up and got better, although I carried the scars for two or three years.

TOMMY GAY

In the camps in Germany, hunger was also rife. For Tommy Gay, a hard day's work on little food was almost too much to endure.

We received half of a loaf of bread every fifth day, German bread, which was very dark, and was more potatoes than anything, I think, and when we went to work we were given a bowl of milky looking potato water, what they had cooked the guards' potatoes in. And if you ate your bread too quickly, then you had to work all the rest of the time with nothing. Sometimes we would be given a loaf between two and either myself or a chum would have to cut it into half. We tied string around each portion and we'd hold it up to check that one didn't weigh a little bit more than the other, and the crumbs; we'd pick them up too so we didn't lose anything.

We did, we'd eat most of our ration there and then and that was lovely to eat a big lump of bread but then, for another three or four days, we'd have none left. We would work until we got too sick. When we came up from the mines we would take our oil lamps to the lamp room. We all carried our own lamps as there was no power down there, no electricity, no torches attached to your helmet; and then the German got his ration of food for the next day and I got nothing, nothing at all and I was starving hungry, you know. Working on an empty belly, it doesn't seem possible, but it was so, that is true, nothing whatever. You would work with the civilian as best you could, try and keep him sweet, it was a miserable life but then he might just give me a little bit of grub, half a sandwich.

FRANK DEANE

The food was muck, the worst was a black soup in which were floating what appeared to be mushrooms or some kind of forest fungus. But you couldn't eat them as they were just like chewing leather and it seemed too that they had just been pulled out of the ground and put into the stewing pot, as they were all full of grit. Then we might get a stew with blobs of what looked like bits of sausage, I couldn't describe the taste, but it was inedible really. There was one ration of bread in the morning, black bread that had to last you all day, and there was coffee which was made of ground acorns. There was so-called tea, too, which was the colour of tea but there seemed to be bits of daisies floating about in it, so what it was made of, I don't know. The Germans didn't have much more than we did, except potatoes, but they can't have been too plentiful as we never saw any of them. If it had not been for Red Cross parcels, we wouldn't have had a chance. I never got any parcels for about two or three months. They had to get the news that you were a prisoner of war to start with, then they had to make arrangements to make up the parcels and send them out, and goodness knows how long they took on the journey, so the long wait was quite understandable. However, we did get a little extra rations from the main parcel headquarters, as some prisoners would die off and their parcels would go into a pool and the food from those would be handed out. We knew prisoners were dying because they were always calling you out to go to somebody's funeral.

FREDERICK HAMMOND

The German food was brown bread made from sawdust and potatoes, then there was supposed to be mangel wurzel soup and goodness alone knows what they put in that, I don't know, dreadful yellow bits and a brown colour. We used to give it to the Russians for doing our washing up, they'd do anything for it because they got no parcels from home. We felt sorry for them, that's why we gave them the food we couldn't eat – not very generous, was it? Still, they were glad of it. The Russians were all bloated, they all had big stomachs because they were so hungry. We used to get parcels every week and bread from Berne. About the second day we got in the hospital, we got Red Cross parcels what they had over from people dying and that, what had been sent out and hadn't

114

been used. The guards on the gate, they'd give anything for a bar of soap or a tin of dripping. In exchange, we'd get eggs from the Germans.

NORMAN COWAN

The rations that the Germans gave us, rye and potato bread, were divided into five sections to be shared by five men. Food was so precious that we made a little balance with a piece of cardboard and string on a stick to weigh it so that one man didn't get a thick slice or a thin slice. We got the food the night before, for the next day, so if you ate the bread straight away you went hungry. We also had a variety of mangel wurzel or carrot soup dug from the fields around the camp, and sauerkraut, which I hated, and barley. Food was cooked in a big cauldron on a fire in the compound for those who did not have any Red Cross parcels. We used to say in very rough language, 'Come on, stir the bloody pot up' so that we might get a little bit of meat or something from the bottom of the cauldron. The men who were captured in the early part of the war, their names were with the Red Cross and they got a parcel every so often, big parcels with all the goodies in. We used to sit and watch them and occasionally they would pass us something. But you felt a bit guilty like, you dropped your pride to take their rations. Some got jobs on the farms. Well, if you got a job on a farm in 1914, 1915, you were landed. The husband was away fighting for the Germans and you were looking after the farm for the rest of the war and getting food. If you milked a cow, you didn't say, 'Germans, take it all', did you? No, you say, 'Let's have a drink.'

ERNIE STEVENS

I was so hungry that I personally exchanged my wristwatch for a slice of their bread and it was very poor quality. Hunger gives you a terrible pain in your stomach. Your stomach is empty, it's got nothing to digest. The natural acids in the stomach have nothing to work on and in time they give you hell. Some people would double up with the pain and try and be sick, but you've got nothing to bring up and that in itself is painful. You're in trouble, very, very, deep trouble. You are at your wits' end trying to make ends meet and don't really notice other people, probably too immersed, too conscious of your own problems. That's what happened, you know, you forget about other people, you're only interested in what's happening to you, it's only natural.

THOMAS SPRIGGS

At Dülmen they gave us some food, a potato or two and soup made from maize that tasted like paraffin; you couldn't eat it. The German cheese, heaven knows what it was made of, but it stank to high heaven, and if you threw it at the wall it would splash and stick to it, it was so poisonous.

At meal times, we would go to the kitchen and collect our rations. I remember the man who looked after the copper, because most of the food was prepared in a copper, and he'd pour something into a bowl for us, bit of potato, bit of fish, occasionally a bit of horse flesh. We would queue up, our bowls in hand, and then he'd ladle whatever he'd made into them, then we'd go back to our beds and eat it.

No, before we got the Red Cross parcels, hunger was always in our thoughts and the fellows were always talking about hunger; what they'd like to eat, marmalade with his bacon, one Merseysider told me he liked. Lancashire fellows used to talk about savoury duck and balm cakes, one Londoner used to talk about doorsteps, thick slices of bread. Food was their chief subject. Men would eat anything, potato peelings, the outer leaves of Brussels sprouts. It was in your mind continually because you were so empty, oh, it was terrible really – hunger, if ever you suffer from it, it's a most unearthly feeling.

JACK ROGERS

The thing is, you couldn't stand up hardly, you had to try and sit down somewhere and there were no armchairs. You had to just sit down on the ground or up against a wall. We looked horrible. We were still wearing the uniforms that we were captured in and they were all beginning to fall to pieces, your shoes too. We didn't get a proper bath, you just tried to wash yourself down a wee bit. In the end, I was in bare feet until a Frenchman managed to get me a pair of sabots. My flesh was hanging loose. It's surprising really where you found strength from. You could feel your bones, all your bones up your arms, round your wrists. I had false teeth then and not even a toothbrush to keep them clean. My cheeks fell in, my face was white and of course the trouble was trying to shave. I was getting very thin all over and weighed about six or seven stones I would guess. It was as much as you could do to walk about, really. Oh, my God, can I tell you what it's like to be hungry? Yes, I can. You feel that you've got nothing inside you. Just like one great empty void and you don't know how you're going to fill it. You get loads of flatulence, wind, you just keep getting filled up with wind because you've got nothing to pass inside you. You keep bringing up wind, bringing up wind, what a state to be in. There's no sort of comfort at all, you can't feel any support of any description, you feel you could drop down any minute, no strength. You used to get these very sudden sharp pains. They double you up, and you don't know what to do. I tried twisting, I tried bending, I tried doing all I could and still all of a sudden you find you just bring wind up and up it comes out of you, gargling out of your throat, oh dear, oh dear. No, it's shocking. There's nothing worse, I think, than being really hungry and of course when you first start to eat you feel almost ravenous and eat too quickly.

NORMAN COWAN

Hunger demoralised the prisoners but it affected the Germans too. Many men, like Norman, recalled how the guards demanded the lifting of the Allied blockade, if the prisoners wished to be properly fed.

You were living on your own fat. I was about eleven stone when I went into the camp and I gradually dropped down to about six stone odd. Hunger is insidious because it makes you open to every disease that there is. In October, there was a big attack of typhus which killed quite a number of men because they couldn't cope with it. In October, sacks of potatoes were brought in and the men, in their eagerness to get them, pushed them into the ashes inside the stove and ate them half raw. Their stomachs could not manage that and so it sort of distended them and killed them.

We used to ask the Germans about the food and they said, 'Well, you tell your navy not to squeeze us, tell them to release their stranglehold and we will feed you.' The Germans were being squeezed to death and retreating, they're not going to give us anything outside the rations, except for a fifth of a loaf of bread, turnip soup and mangel wurzels and meat when available, but very seldom. It's vivid in my mind. If they've hardly got any food, do you think they'd give it to prisoners of war?

PERCY WILLIAMS

The Germans never hit us, there were never any physical attacks, but they used to curse us, 'bloody Schweinehunde'.

118

The interpreter used to tell us that it was our problem that we had no clothes or proper food. 'You Schweinehund, it's your fault, you're not allowing any food to come into the country, we are hard up, we're starving, the children are hungry, you are the aggressors, therefore you deserve what you get.' They said there were no clothes in the country, there was no leather, soap, or fats to be had because of the blockade. The Germans told us they were fighting a righteous war; that God was on their side.

JACK ROGERS

If men like Jack ever forgot about their hunger, it was usually because they were after a prized cigarette.

One thing we missed was a smoke. Some of the Frenchmen had been prisoners since 1914 and they had all sorts of packages coming out, including tobacco and newspapers. They used to roll some tobacco in a paper and make a cigarette. One or two of them would walk along with a fat bit of tobacco, smoking. Well, of course, we hadn't got anything like that so we used to follow them, me and another chap, and wait and hope that when they'd finished, they'd drop their cigarettes so we could pick them up. But they never did. Every time they finished smoking, they'd drop the butt and put their foot on it and pick it up and put it in their pocket. Eventually, a family friend, Mrs Addis, sent me out about fifty cigarettes and my gosh, did I have some friends. The men would do anything for a smoke, some men used to go crackers for it, would pinch anything to get some.

PERCY WILLIAMS

The Germans used to smoke Turkish cigars, horrible things they were – and then they'd throw their stub ends over the wire, these Jerries, these bloody square heads, they used to think it very funny that these poor buggers would scramble for a fag, for a cigar end. The lads who smoked were so desperate for a fag, they used to gather up the leaves in the autumn, cut them up, and with a bit of newspaper make them into a cigarette and have a smoke.

CHAPTER SIX

The Gift of Life

It is no exaggeration to say that thousands of British prisoners who survived the Great War would have died had
they not received regular parcels of food. The provision of
food parcels became an industry and proved to be an international lifeline for men who would have died either of
outright starvation or, more likely, an illness they were too
weak to combat.

Their survival, indeed often their comfort, was due to a
multitude of organisations which were set up from the start
of the war to provide not only basic relief but comforts to
British soldiers imprisoned in Germany. The Salvation Army,
the YMCA, Regimental and charitable Help Committees,
and the soldier's own family provided a network of support
that became so large and at times unwieldy that many
soldiers were overwhelmed with generous donations from
home. It was an operation that, by 1916, had to be rationalised
under one central organising authority, the International Red
Cross.

The packages sent to prisoners were generally of two types,
food or clothing. The images of soldiers wearing distinctive
dark blue uniforms taken in camp photographs, show men
not in uniforms provided by the Germans but in clothes sent
from Britain, replacing tattered or worn out khaki. They came
in separate parcels and at different times, a tunic, a pair of
boots, socks and underwear; a prisoner gradually building up
his uniform so that it is not unusual to see pictures of
prisoners dressed half in their old khaki, half in a new
uniform.

A food parcel was designed to weigh 13lbs and registered soldiers could expect to receive two every fortnight. In them they would find a multitude of foodstuffs including cocoa, tea, cigarettes, bully beef, biscuits, cheese, tinned milk and dripping. Bread, which was baked at home, was also available, but such was the delay in its transportation that bakeries were set up in neutral countries to ensure quicker distribution. So well fed were many soldiers that they were able to give up eating German food, many happily passing on their allowance to starving Russian soldiers, either for nothing or in exchange for jobs done around the huts, including cleaning and washing.

German guards, like German soldiers at the front, envied the quantity and quality of foodstuffs received by British prisoners, the disparity between the warring nations growing wider as the conflict ground on. Such was the effect of the Allied blockade on German ports, and so great the economic and industrial mismanagement at home, that many camp guards brokered deals between themselves and prisoners, exchanging fresh fruit or vegetables for tinned food or fats, such as soap. It meant that for those prisoners in the best camps, life, while never rosy, was at least bearable.

Yet parcels sent do not equal parcels received. To be a recipient, a prisoner had to be registered as being in one of the camps or many Kommandos in Germany or France. In theory, the German Government was responsible for passing on lists of prisoners to the International Red Cross, who in turn would pass on the details to the British authorities. Soldiers, too, were issued with small blue cards, filled out on capture and sent back home to relatives, not only informing them that they were alive and well, but in turn letting their regiments and the military authorities know that they were no longer missing. Germany provided this information on a reciprocal basis with Britain. It was a system that worked, to a degree.

But not all prisoners were given cards. Not all were able to write letters home, not all were able to meet delegations of the

Red Cross that periodically toured camps taking notes and writing down unregistered names. Even when registered, the information took weeks to be processed, by which time a prisoner could well have been moved to another camp, or to a work Kommando, his first parcel lagging well behind. This cumbersome administration meant that at main parent camps undelivered packets or parcels became stockpiled, each one carrying a label addressed to a man sent elsewhere or who had perhaps died. At one camp, Soltau, the numbers of undelivered packets reached astronomical proportions by 1918, with some 200,000 packets warehoused. These parcels were not always wasted but were, on occasions, handed out or shared among new prisoners as they awaited their own parcels, but this happened at the better camps and was not automatic.

The distribution of packages was not regulated and depended on the nature of the camp regime. In the better camps, Allied prisoners were often put to work in packet rooms administering the handover of packages under the watchful eye of German supervisors. In many brutal camps this never happened, with packages being stored up by the guards and released, often article by article, to prisoners only after thorough inspection. The problem, in part, had been Allied-made. Early on in the war there had been cases of files or small saws being hidden in food packages, compasses dropped into cans of soup and maps concealed in wrapping, all done to effect a prisoner's escape. This had made commandants wary, particularly those whose camps were close to Germany's borders. However, the distribution of packages was slow and not just for reasons of security. Jealousy, carelessness, tardiness, vindictiveness, theft, incompetence: they all played a part in explaining why many prisoners never saw their food parcels.

It may seem surprising that food parcels were allowed to reach prisoners at all, when German civilians were starving. However, to a certain extent foreign food aid helped take the pressure off the Germans, who were struggling not only to feed their own people, but also the prisoners who, from early on in the war, had numbered two million. It would have been difficult, too, for the Germans to ignore the international outrage that would have accompanied any decision to halt food convoys. For most of the war the Germans had one eye on American public opinion, and could not afford to alienate the United States, should news cross the Atlantic that Allied soldiers were being starved to death. The Germans had prisoners in Britain who were adequately fed but who still received comfort parcels. It would have been in no one's interest if, in retaliation, the British had halted these.

At the camps, food parcels were a god-send to the prisoners and they were a god-send to those guarding them too. For an unscrupulous commandant, parcels could be stockpiled or rationed so as to exert pressure and exact obedience from prisoners. For a guard it could mean an extra, and vital, source of food for himself and the family. There is no doubt that parcels were stolen from prisoners, human temptation was too great and in some camps the opportunity too ripe to miss. It was easy, and even understandable, for guards to blame the blockade for their misery. Theft was easily justified when, at camps such as Sennelager, women and children were seen begging for food close to the barbed wire. It meant that once parcels began arriving, prisoners tended to be as much resigned as resentful at having items pinched, knowing as most did that the guards had little to eat themselves. It was a fact of life and a necessary evil, if that's what it took to win a war.

PERCY WILLIAMS

The news that Percy Williams had been captured was vitally important, not just for allaying family fears at home, but in order that he could be registered for food parcels.

For weeks, my parents had no idea what had happened and this worried me. The Germans did not take our details until July, so all the information my parents received was that I had been reported missing. I did meet a friend from home, Jack Jones from Llandrindod Wells. He'd been captured with the Durham Light Infantry and I gave him my mother's address and he gave me his. We said that as soon as ever we could, we would write to each other's family. However, not until I was in Germany, through my parent POW camp at Limburg, was I allowed to write on a special card to send through to Switzerland. It said that Private Williams 757273, 5th Northumberland Fusiliers, was a prisoner of war in Germany and that I was alive and only slightly wounded. We were kept in France for at least two months, so my parents knew nothing until at least August and of course they feared the worst; mother, I learnt later, was demented with worry for weeks and weeks.

FRANK DEANE

My parents didn't know I was a prisoner for two or three months. They knew I was missing, they'd been told that. I was out in the fresh air at Kassel one day up against a cage, and on the other side of the cage was one of our officers. I don't know if he recognised me or not, but we had a bit of a chat and he said he would try and get a message to England that I was actually a prisoner of war, so my parents got to know a little bit earlier than they might have done. He was Lt Giles of first platoon, I think. I was in second platoon.

JACK ROGERS

I'd been a prisoner for about three or four months but my parents at home had no idea where I was. They only had a notice from the War Office to say I was missing, believed prisoner, and that's all they could tell them. It wasn't until the Danish Red Cross visited our camp and took down the names and regiments of all the prisoners that were there, that news reached my folks that I was really alive. The Germans hadn't notified anyone that I know of.

We were in a pretty bad state, I can assure you. You can imagine the relief when the first parcels from the Red Cross started to come through. A friend at home discovered through the Danish Red Cross that I was a prisoner at the camp and got me onto the official prisoners of war list at home, and so I began to receive Red Cross parcels.

NORMAN COWAN

I never received any parcels because I was missing, believed killed, 42843, me. They never knew at home because I never received any letters at all. 42843, as far as the army was concerned, as far as the Red Cross was concerned, I was dead. Many, many men didn't get parcels, so they had to survive as far as they could, some by pinching, some by learning to eat things they'd never eaten before. The French ate cats. They ate cats!

WALTER HUMPHRYS

Ever since capture, Walter had been working behind the German lines. Without food parcels, surviving on German rations was at the very least problematic. For prisoners in France or in Germany, stealing food was a dangerous but often necessary course of action.

We worked on a food dump at first, carrying rice and potatoes, oats, salt and tins of meat to a village to keep us and our guards fed. At first, it was fairly easy to steal food-stuffs including flour and oats which, when formed into cakes, made an indigestible but filling food. Sometimes there would be a hole in the sack and when the guard's back was turned we'd pinch a bit of whatever it held, but you risked the stick if you were seen. The Germans soon found out and we were all searched every day when we left the dump, offenders being thrashed and sometimes imprisoned. I got the stick twice: once whilst I was carrying sacks of oats, a German officer struck me on the head, and on another occasion I was hit when I was found to have hidden some food in the palm of my hand under an old glove.

JACK ROGERS

There was a prison next door for punishment, and you'd see men frog-marched around the camp with a pack on their back, bent double. Heaven knows how long they kept that up for. One of the jobs was sowing tiny new potatoes which we carried in our upturned shirts, dropping the spud into the groove made by the plough we were following. At the end, there would be quite a few potatoes left, well, if you could you'd try and pinch a few, tucking them under your shirt. If a German happened to spot that you looked too fat, he'd touch you and if he found you'd been pinching potatoes, then you were punished.

THOMAS SPRIGGS

Once the German offensive started, we were taken to a village near Le Vain where we worked in the quartermaster stores, boxing or bagging up rations for the German regiments billeted near by. They'd only got a few potatoes there and a drink that they'd brewed, called Schnapps, which, I guess, was, for the Germans, like the rum we got in the trenches. Well, we got at this stuff. There was a fellow there called Thomas, and he'd got a pal there from the Manchester area, and Thomas got quite tight on this Schnapps. However, we got him back to the camp without the Germans noticing and onto one of the top bunks. Now he wanted to relieve himself and there was an empty bottle there, which he used, and an hour or so later his pal was talking to me and he said, 'What was in that bottle by Thomas' bed?' And I said that he'd relieved himself because he was too tight to get up and go to the latrine, and this fellow said, 'I had a drink of it and I thought it had a queer taste.' He didn't seem that bothered about it at all.

At this camp near Le Vain, as you walked down the road and turned the corner into the compound there was a little wicket gate and on this corner was a latrine, the usual type, pole across a trench and boarded up so far and open at the top. We used to try to steal, or should I say purloin, perhaps a potato or whatever we could get our hands on, carrying it in our crutch. Anyway the Germans must have got wind that something had been stolen and they were going to search us when we got back to the camp, but as we passed the latrine, one of the fellows who'd got a tin lobbed it over straight into the pit. He waited a couple of hours, the Germans searched and found nothing, then he returned, fished this tin out, washed it, opened it and ate the contents.

FRANK DEANE

One of the rooms in the house we were in was used to store onions. There wasn't a door but there was a barricade half way up, and if you got a stick with a nail on the end you could spear an onion now and then, which would improve the stew. Sometimes we would have to take bags of potatoes into the store of the manager's house which was quite close by, and if you were quick and the guard was out of sight, you could nick a couple of potatoes which you would shove under your mattress. You got quite ingenious dodging the attentions of the Germans.

PERCY WILLIAMS

By October it was very, very cold. We were living in an old warehouse and there was no heating. We were absolutely frozen and we used to sleep close together so as to keep warm. We had little underclothing, we just wore a shirt, underpants, trousers, socks and clogs on our feet. On Sunday, we used to have to wash our clothes in cold water, no soap, and try and get them dry, otherwise they would be wet for the next day. I thought if we could get some wood, we would be able to warm ourselves and we could get dry. The area was heavily wooded and the Germans had cut up some wood and brought it into the camp and stacked it up. It was forbidden to touch it, but myself and a friend, a man called Hughes, we took a chance and stole some wood on a couple of occasions. We were given away by some Russians, who had been accused of stealing the wood themselves, the result being we were given two days' solitary confinement on bread and water as a punishment.

JACK ROGERS

In the bigger camps, inspections by neutral observers were designed to find out and note down the details of new arrivals, while at the same time ensuring that existing prisoners were fed and treated properly. At Münster I, Jack Rogers recalled one visit, and how ineffective it was.

By making an application to the Germans, the Danish Red Cross were allowed to pay a visit to our camp on one occasion, a Sunday I think it was. About seven or eight observers were to see all the huts and have a look at what we were being fed, so of course the Germans laid on everything they possibly could. Outside the cook house they placed a menu for the day, with our food chalked up on the board. We'd never had a menu before of any sort. We had diced and baked potatoes and a dixie full of stuff they called 'Reisgriess', semolina we'd call it. Anyway, we had a dish each of these which was quite a big meal, all designed to impress the watching Red Cross that Jerry was doing all he could for us. They weren't really allowed to ask any questions about how we were being treated, because the Germans were always standing watching and listening. The visitors would ask, 'Are you all right?' in a vague sort of way, so you had to tell them your food was adequate, that we were doing fairly well and that we were comfortable. On no occasion were we allowed to be alone with them. There were always these Germans present, listening and waiting and looking at you and in a sense threatening you. So you daren't really say anything other than 'Yes, thanks very much – yes, no, thank you, yes.' You're absolutely afraid. I mean the Germans couldn't take much away in the manner of food, could they, else we shouldn't have got any at all. So if we had complained, we would have been punished behind the prison walls, slowly walking around with a pack of bricks or stones on your back, doubled up almost in half.

ERNIE STEVENS

Many prisoners like Ernie knew about camp observers but never saw them. How the Red Cross came to hear about his captivity was irrelevant to Ernie, so long as he received a parcel. Its arrival was an answer to a prayer.

The parcels were a blessing, I shared mine with a pal and he shared his with me. Other people did the same, sometimes three or four in a group. I remember one Scotsman, he was a funny guy and wouldn't share his parcel with anybody just in case they had a little more than he did. There was a postcard in every parcel that we had to fill out and send back to England so they knew whether our parcels had arrived. Mine took a long time to come through, from April to about September, but nevertheless when they came it was a joyous occasion, believe me. The parcels first went to our parent camp, Münster I, then they were sent on to us. To get some food, we had to go to the parcel office where we gave our names and number, '121 Stevens' and ask for a tin of this, a package of that and a man would go to our place on the shelf and pick out a can. We didn't have the whole parcel to ourselves, whereas I believe in other camps the parcels were handed over to the prisoner whole. However, in our camp the Germans insisted on holding on to the packet. When we wanted a tin, they'd fetch it, then stab the top with a knife, so they could be sure that there was nothing untoward inside that might help us in an escape. Small packages they would feel, then hand over to us. In the past, people had had parcels straight from home and of course there was always a way of hiding a compass, a file, or a map in the contents. Now, I understand, the Red Cross made arrangements with the Germans that nothing would be put in the food that would aid us in escaping.

JACK ROGERS

We used to get two or three parcels every two or three weeks, or were supposed to receive them. They got as far as the railway station, piled up all along the platforms. Then some Germans would take a party of us down there with a hand-cart and collect them, dragging the cart back to our camp. They only allowed us so many parcels each time. Most were left behind, so instead of getting perhaps three a fortnight, we sometimes only got one, you see. Well, that meant there were two of my parcels still standing there at the station, accumulating with all the rest. It was just a bit of spite. When we got back to the camp, the Germans called us out on parade, the interpreter standing on the cart shouting out the names and numbers. These parcels might have articles of clothing in them or they might have food. One of the pictures I have, we are all dressed in black, well, they were clothes we received from home. Those parcels would contain some food or articles of clothing, so you'd begin to have a new pair of shoes or a cap or a jacket and trousers, then perhaps an undershirt. I doubt if we could have survived without them, we were getting so thin. I'll tell you, it was the British Red Cross that absolutely kept us going, definitely. When the parcels came through, we got quite a lot of tins. We were beginning to get lovely chunks of roast beef inside us, solid food, but there was a reaction. After drinking all this filthy cooking juice, all of a sudden better food started to send everybody out in boils, boils all over the place. Boils all round your neck, boils around your arms, your legs, behind your knees. There was no medicine so prisoners had to wait and wait until they began to burst. I had one great big boil in the centre of the back of my neck and I used to have to walk around with my head bowed. I didn't know what to do so I used to dip a rag in some hot tea and dab the boil until it broke, what a relief. But some chaps ended up in hospital covered with them.

TOMMY GAY

Our parcels were heaven – and two loaves of bread from a neutral country, Holland or Denmark. We would get 200 fags, a tin of bully beef, cheese, half a pound of chocolate, tea, sugar, a packet of biscuits, beautiful, all in a little compact box, couldn't go wrong. There were Russians there who didn't even get half the German loaf, so I took one on as a friend and every time I had my tea, he would share my grub. I called this man Alec and he came from the Ukraine, where he worked as a jeweller. I'd get my parcel and I might have a tin of salmon, for instance, so I'd cut the bread, a couple of slices, and Alec and I would have a little tea party. One day he said, 'Tell one of these Germans that you work with to get you a bit of aluminium if you can and bring it to me'. I managed to get a bit from one of the friendlier Germans and Alec took this piece of brass and made a ring to fit my finger on top of which he engraved a small cross. I was very proud of the ring, as I am now, I think a hell of a lot of it and it's on my finger now and it reminds me of years and years ago, a reminder every day of my life, and it never moves. He was a friend and I was happy to meet him and to make him a friend.

When our parcels came up on the railway, we could see them arriving, in box vans with bolts and six or seven big padlocks on the wagons, so that no German could break in and steal them. It was no surprise at all that people were dying of starvation because we were all more or less hungry. But we were living like lords, absolutely, when we got our Red Cross parcels.

THOMAS SPRIGGS

Food was bad until we got the Red Cross parcels, then we got biscuits and soup, chocolate, cigarettes, dripping, cake and soap. They were a godsend. I remember that tin of dripping because I tucked into it the first day we got the parcels and it made me feel a bit sick afterwards. I suppose my stomach couldn't take too much greasy food at once. I suppose if we hadn't had the Red Cross parcels we would have starved to death eventually, very, very gradually.

The Germans gave us a card to say that we were prisoners of war and I suppose from then on, mother and my sisters got busy and got in touch with the Red Cross, and eventually got the parcels through. They were sixteen to eighteen inches square, brown cardboard with a name and prisoner of war number on it. You could see if they had been tampered with and some of the stuff removed. If there was a chance to take any of this food out of the parcels, they would do – can you blame them? I remember being on parade when they were given out and our numbers and names were called and we went up and collected it, I think I got about four parcels in all in the first batch.

ERNIE STEVENS

Because we didn't know what was in these packages, we had no way of telling whether we were getting everything that had been sent. How many tins did we have? How many packages of tea, coffee, cocoa, powdered milk? It was impossible to know whether any were being stolen or given to somebody else, but I can assure you there did not seem to be much in the way of contents for what was a substantial parcel. I am as sure as sure can be that we did not get all that was sent to us. Absolutely, I wouldn't trust them half an inch. I guarantee that most of the stuff in those parcels disappeared. There was nothing to stop the Germans helping themselves, and they were short of food and it was a great temptation. I suppose, in a sense, a lot of our troubles were due to the British blockade, but that was the price we had to pay in order to win the war. Nevertheless, if they had come round, I was ready to tell the International Red Cross that this was going on, but while they used to go to the big camps, they rarely visited small places like ours.

THOMAS SPRIGGS

Quite a number of the parcels were stolen and never did get to us, although quite a few got through as well. We knew roughly what should have been in them and we could see that the boxes had been tampered with, that someone had been through them. Once, we had to follow a sergeant to the station who was about to go home on leave. Two of us carried his bag to the train and we said to one another, he's got a lot of our stuff in that bag, it is much too heavy for ordinary clothing. Through the material we could feel the tins in there and it proved to us that it was every man for himself in the camp.

FRANK DEANE

There were two sets of parcels, individual and ones that were for general use to help men who hadn't received anything up to that point. They were sometimes a bit battered when we got them, and I did think some may have been tampered with. The Germans, of course, may have stolen the parcels in transit before they got into British hands, not on a wholesale basis but I'm quite sure individual Germans did, I mean, you couldn't really blame them as they were half starved. It was a natural thing for people to do who were not entirely honest. We knew that things were sometimes pilfered from the parcels, we could tell that things had been messed about a bit with the packing. We talked about it to each other and, I mean, what was the army made of? All sorts of criminals and odd bods and we were bound to have a few people who stole. In fact, one of the eye openers being in that army was all the different people you had as comrades, and I found I got on well with most of them from all walks of life. We had miners and policemen and steelworkers, a bank clerk. Many clubbed together and would share the same stew and the parcels, just two or three men together. The bank clerk was the only one I rather disliked, a superior sort of fellow. He was in a little group who shared their rations, and another man left the group because he felt this chap was trying to swindle them.

Stealing went on from the parcels, in fact I think whole

135

parcels went from time to time, taken from the shop where they were held. Just after the Armistice, there was a fire in the packet shop and I always thought it was a fire that had been engineered so that the records would be destroyed; but that was purely an assumption on my part.

CHAPTER SEVEN

Last Days

The prisoners captured in the spring offensive of 1918 had the first inkling of any Allied troops that all in the German Army was not well. Once they were taken behind the front lines, the prisoners were surprised at the ramshackle state of the Army's war machine, with half-starved horses pulling wagons and sixteen year old boys in uniform. It alerted them to the fact that while Stormtroopers might be cutting swathes through the Allied lines, it was a violent assault that had little to support it.

When the offensive broke down in the summer of 1918, the turnaround was quick and decisive. The Allied armies inexorably pushed the Germans back, and with the retreat went the prisoners, marching from one village to another, halting perhaps for a week or two, then later, as the war drew to a close, stopping for no more than a day or two. After years of trench warfare, the stalemate had been broken and the war had become one of movement. Slogging along the roads, the prisoners found themselves accompanied by civilians, for villages which had been relative backwaters behind the enemy lines now became the targets for front line action. It was reminiscent of 1914, when, during the retreat from Mons, civilians had clogged the roads, carrying every item of personal property that could be slung on a wagon or hoisted onto shoulders.

At the POW camps in Germany, news of the fighting was obtained sporadically, but even as early as September the rumours were consistent about Allied advances and the fact that the enemy was losing the war. For those in the best camps, with food parcels to keep them going, it was just a matter of hanging on until peace was declared. For many other prisoners, however, peace could not come soon enough. The flu epidemic that was sweeping Europe was killing off prisoners at an alarming rate, as most were too weak or sick to put up any resistance. Even among those who were not struck down, the gradual erosion of their health through work and neglect made many desperate for the war to end. For those men of 1914 who had been imprisoned and neglected for four years, their physical state was pitiful, one recalling how a comrade, shortly before he died, had turned to eating the lice that crawled across his clothes.

In a few camps and in many Kommandos the arrival of food parcels began to break down as the German transportation network crumbled. If there could be said to be one positive aspect, it was that, as Germany teetered on the brink of civil war, the more brutal guards and commandants toned down their aggression. With one eye on possible post-war retribution, many guards became conspicuous by their absence. When the war finished, most camp guards simply disappeared; they didn't all leave simply because their services were no longer required.

GEORGE GADSBY

George had been one of the many thousands of prisoners who had been shunted from one village to another, working for the Germans in France and Belgium. Now, in the last months of the war, he was ideally placed to watch the slow disintegration of the German army.

About this time, great excitement began to prevail, and the hospitals at Cambrai gradually became packed with wounded. It was quite a daily occurrence to see parties of 60 to 100 wounded Germans tramping along to hospital, evidently walking all the way from the firing line. As our Allies advanced, the town became the scene of great aeroplane activity, and we gazed from the barrack room window at many a lively encounter when two and sometimes three machines came to earth. We did not mind them coming when we were at work, as the Germans always hurried us to the cellars as quickly as they could and thereby gave us a rest from our labour.

Towards the end of August, the Germans began making preparations for the defence of Cambrai and began massing their transport as near as they could to our billets, thinking they would be safe. The first day, 'Tommy' came over in broad daylight and deposited bombs just in the roadway at the gate of our enclosure, killing several Germans and smashing the transport to atoms.

Bombing developed so much that it became particularly dangerous to us, and we had to seek shelter in the cellars, but although bombs fell inside our enclosure and near the gate, fortunately we had no casualties. The most memorable bombing incident occurred when our aeroplanes, taking advantage of an early morning mist, deposited bombs on three munitions trains waiting in Cambrai station. I was in the dye works when the explosions began and I was escorted to a somewhat dilapidated shelter where we remained for a couple of hours listening to a typical front line barrage. During the explosions a ration store was demolished, and needless to say our more fortunate comrades, who had to help extricate the stores from the burning building, performed meritorious rescues of soup powders, jam, grease, biscuits, cigarettes and cigars, which they managed to bring away with them, hidden in the insides of their shirts and trousers.

We could witness Allied shells bursting at Bourlon Wood, so on the 5th of September we had to pack up as quickly as we could and commence retreating with the Germans. The roads were packed with transport, guns and men, entering

Cambrai. After a tiresome march of 20 miles, we arrived at a new temporary premises at Trith St Leger. We had completed five months' work at Cambrai but the Germans did not derive anything from it as they left it too late to transport the iron to the furnaces of Germany. On the 7th of September whilst we were staying at Trith St Leger, my first parcel, which was posted on the 5th of May, arrived. This was not only a great relief as regards food but it certified that my people knew that I was a prisoner although I had received no communication from them since the 16th of March.

During our stay there, we picked up several pamphlets dropped from our aeroplanes giving us details of the Italian victory on the Piave and our great advance on the Cambrai sector. We began to see that the war was almost at an end. We also understood that matters were very serious with the Germans, as the roads were busily occupied with retreating transport. It became almost a daily occurrence for some German officer to remark 'The war finish, Tommy', as he passed on the road with his worn column.

It was pitiful to watch the unfortunate civilians pass by. They were compelled to evacuate their homes as they came under the fire of the advancing allied guns. Old ladies could be seen carrying heavy loads on their backs, women of middle age wheeling barrows heavily laden with bedding, furniture and so on, children from three years of age carrying kettles or any sundry articles and mothers carrying babies, and, at the same time, their share of household belongings. The Germans never offered to help them, and the distances they had to walk were anything from 10 to 16 miles, as they had to reach the next large town before they could obtain food.

The retreat went on. By early October we had crossed over into Belgium. Here the Germans allowed the Belgians to bring us vegetables and food to our billet, chiefly because they themselves were practically starving and wanted a share of what the civilians had to offer us. We continued our journey the next day, the civilians providing us with ample food wherever we went, we being the first Britishers they had seen since 1914.

When passing through Binche we were simply held up by the civilians. They came from everywhere bringing us soup, cake, bread, coffee, milk, cigarettes and cigars. I think they must have known the war was practically over as they seemed to be giving us their hidden stores. We endeavoured to struggle up a steep hill but we could not move for the children. The youngsters were clinging to our necks, cutting off our buttons. A typical Prussian sergeant came out and tried to move the crowd but he had to retire, being cowed by the 'booing' of little children.

We reached Fontaine L'Evêque where we were now to stay until the evening of the Armistice. Our billets were in a large building which had once been the scene of great commercial activity, but here as in France, the Germans had removed all the machinery to Germany. The floor was concrete and the wall at the far end of the factory had been knocked down in order to enable the Germans to extricate the machinery. We had to sleep on the floor with just a little straw to place under our tired and aching limbs. The Belgians owning the factory fetched a stove and erected it and supplied us with coal. A Belgian lady and two English ladies, who had been unable to get away in 1914, brought us some hot soup. The mayor of the town also provided us with a small loaf of bread and a little lard for each soldier.

Unfortunately, the majority of our party contracted influenza. No German doctor was able to visit us. A Medical Corps sergeant visited us every three days but he could not obtain medicine to give us. Many of our fellow prisoners were carried to hospital in a critical condition, two suffering from internal haemorrhage. The Belgians brought in a civilian doctor who declared that the medicine we had ought to be placed on a fire after which the Germans stopped him from coming. The consequence was that 30 out of 100 were taken to hospital and many of them, I am afraid, would not last very long. I had rather bad attacks that necessitated my being confined to a bed for a fortnight but thanks to a Belgian who brought me special food and two eggs, I made a sufficient recovery to walk with the last of my comrades on our retreating journey towards Namur. We had an exciting march as our aeroplanes dropped bombs which fell a little too near to be enjoyed.

NORMAN COWAN

October 1918 was a disastrous month in the POW camps and was fatal for many of the prisoners. The main cause was typhus fever which spread from the Russian to the French and British compounds. It was very infectious, many prisoners falling into a coma or becoming very weak physically. The unsanitary conditions and a big lice infection were responsible.

Apart from our poor physical condition, we were in poor mental state. I was glad to be out of the war, so you would say to yourself 'I'm in a prisoner of war camp, I've got to make the best of it. I'm alive, and therefore if I carry on I might get home.' We knew the war was nearly over because we had a chap in our camp who'd been a teacher and could speak three languages. The French had been there a long time and they had smuggled in newspapers. This man went down to the French compound and would come back with news of what was happening. We knew the Germans, we began to realise that they were losing the war. That meant that you were prepared to stand what was happening in the hope that you would get home. You accept what's going on, knowing the men at the front are fighting, that they are doing their best for you, that you're going to win. That buoyed us up.

ERNIE STEVENS

Even though the war was nearing its end, many prisoners were still determined to escape. Unable to stand incarceration any longer, or simply driven by patriotic fervour, prisoners like Ernie plotted a quick get-away to neutral Holland.

At a meeting that every platoon in England attended, when we were first called up, we had to listen to a senior officer telling us that if we were captured we were to make life as awkward for the enemy as we possibly could. If anybody escaped, that's a good thing because hundreds of German troops would be looking for us, keeping them busy. I tried my best in that regard. I embraced the idea! I would not accept my imprisonment but would make trouble for the enemy. I never took to the fact that the Kaiser, who started this war against his grandmother's country, was nice and proper at all. I didn't like it, so the idea of escaping was put into my head before I even left England.

JACK ROGERS

Despite his proximity to Holland, Jack was typical of others who were physically too weak to effect an escape.

We all thought about escaping and, had I felt fitter and had more strength, I might have made the attempt like one or two others. We weren't far from Holland but I was too weak physically, and unable to go and travel even a short distance on practically nothing to eat, so it was useless trying. For a while all we wore were wooden clogs anyway and it was months before the Red Cross parcels we received helped us regain any of the strength we had lost. No, the only hope I had of getting home was to try and hang on as long as I could where I was.

ERNIE STEVENS

At Dülmen camp I made a good friend called Sid Stillwell. Most men chummed up with at least one other person. He was still wearing his cap and I noticed the badge was of the same regiment as my father had been in and that attracted me to him. We shared our parcels and we worked together from the start, breaking up the limestone. We were sitting together one day and I had wondered whether to say anything to him about escaping. When I spoke to him he seemed a bit surprised but thought it was a good idea. I told him I had been given directions from a Frenchman in the camp who had tried to escape himself but had been caught. I told Sid that from my Red Cross parcels I had received everything I'd needed in the way of clothes and was only anxiously awaiting my boots. Any escape depended on these boots arriving because I couldn't escape without them as my army ones were falling to pieces.

These new boots arrived on the 25th September and I said to Sid that we would try that night. We had saved six or seven bars of chocolate from our parcels and some biscuits to keep us going. We worked that evening loaded up with food, keeping our overcoats on to hide any bulges. I wondered whether the Germans would notice, but they didn't keep their eye on us specifically nor ask any questions. Holland was only twenty miles away. All we had to do was get across a large field and then hit the main road south towards Geldern. We took our escape very, very seriously. This was my life, because we could easily have a bullet in the back, very easily, from one of the guards at the factory, at the frontier, or anyone in between.

To escape from the factory would not be difficult, far easier than any camp where there was barbed wire all around. We would wait until the night shift and then during our first break, which was at eight o'clock, we'd get away. The powerful arc lights lit only the area under the roof, and under there of course the light was very bright. I'd go and get a pail of water from a standpipe and a few seconds later Sid would ask permission to go to the toilet. Now both of these spots were just outside the range of the lights, so we would be temporarily in darkness. I turned the tap on so that they could hear the noise of the water running. Usually you would run the tap for a moment anyway to make sure the water was clean, then you'd rinse out the pail before filling it, so that all gave us time. As soon as Sid caught up with me, we both, as quickly as we could, climbed over three or four very high piles of screened coal. Sliding down with the coal on the far side, we got over the wall of the factory, ran across the road, and into a field and through a hedge.

When we went through the hedge there was a couple courting on the far side and we frightened the wits out of them and we were a bit scared ourselves, I must admit. We heard them gasp but we didn't hang about. Later, after we got onto the Geldern Road, we heard a motorcycle coming up behind us; it was some distance away then so we dived into a ditch. It was very wet by that time and our overcoats were sodden, so when he had passed we got up and it was getting towards dawn then and so we got into a forest. Each of us picked a tree, climbed up and got into a fork in the branches and slept during the day and when I woke up my clothes were dry. When it was dark we set off again on the road towards Geldern. I had been told by the Frenchman that when we got to the outskirts of that town we had to make a right turn which would lead us to the frontier.

It was evening when we reached Geldern. We were on the pavement on the left-hand side of the road when all of a sudden on the opposite side came half a dozen German soldiers. They might have just come out of a pub for all I know. There were just two or three footsteps and there they were. As they got quite near us, I guess there must have been an NCO amongst them, as they made an 'eyes right' and saluted us, and we, of course, returned the salute and walked

145

on. They thought we were officers, German officers! Of course our prison uniforms were unlike the normal uniforms either British or German soldiers would wear.

At a certain point we took a right turn and it was only about half a mile and there was the canal and the frontier we were looking for. First of all, we tried to cross over the canal but directly we put our feet on the boards of the footbridge a dog started barking, so that stopped us crossing there. We walked on, Sid ahead, when unfortunately he got onto a pebble pathway next to the canal. As he walked along you could hear him a mile off, he was making an awful noise and I thought, 'Why the dickens don't you get off the path?' But I dare not shout out at all because my voice would carry in that clear night air. I was obviously a little more conscious of things, I was walking on grass, you couldn't hear me at all. I was some yards behind him and it wasn't very long, just a matter of seconds really, before I heard, 'Halt! Hands up' and I thought, "Oh heavens, he's walked into a German sentry".' It was all over as far as Sid was concerned. Sure enough, he had been caught less than fifty yards away from safety in Holland. I went flat on the ground and watched. There was just that interval when I thought about going to help Sid, but then the German did what he was supposed to do; he blew a whistle for other guards to come from the hut with dogs. I could faintly make out the dog but it didn't even smell me or look my way, fortunately.

We had decided beforehand that if one was caught, the other should get away if he could, but I didn't want to see Sid go through punishment on his own. I felt sure that if I gave myself up and was in the same prison, that it would be a comfort to him, and me and he would be able to stick it out a little better than if he was on his own. Within fifteen minutes I got up and walked towards them and gave myself up. The guards took us to their hut which was on the same road, running parallel to the frontier and in there we stayed the night. During the evening I asked permission to go to the toilet. One of the sentries took me outside and he whispered, 'You be heimat by Weihnachten, Deutschland ist kaput.' I didn't know what Weihnachten meant at the time but afterwards it turned out that he'd said I would be home by Christmas. Germany was finished.

In the morning, we were taken from the guard's hut. It was then that I saw the number of cans strung up between bushes and trees at ankle, waist and chest height with just a pebble or two inside, even in a breeze they were shaking. I knew it would have been very difficult for me to get away, so I was glad I did what I did and gave myself up. From the hut we were taken to a police station cell, in a town called Kevelaer. There were about six cells in a row and the last but one cell had 'Kriegsgefangene' or 'war prisoners' over the door, so they evidently had a good business going there.

We spent about ten or twelve days lying on mattresses in those cells before two sentries from our parent camp, Münster I, arrived to take us back. When they first came, they told us to open our tunics and take our braces off. The idea was that we would have to have our hands in our pockets to hold our trousers up, ensuring we couldn't run away. They then took us off to the station and back to our camp near the factory. When we arrived, we had to go into the sentries' hut which was just inside the gate. Just as the gate closed behind us, one of the sentries there appeared and he was as mad as a hatter. He had his bayonet fixed to his rifle and he came up to me and started yelling, oh it went on for a good couple of minutes, swearing in German, and then he pointed his bayonet at the middle of my stomach, which I did not appreciate. The tip of the bayonet was as near going into my skin as it's possible to get. Evidently he was one of those on duty when we had taken a walk and had no doubt been hauled over the coals. 'He's going to stick this in me unless I do something,' I thought. So I rounded on him and said, 'Hey you, when the English come, the military police, they will get you and string you up,' and I motioned as if to show him hanging by a rope. Do you know, his face went all kind of colours and he turned on his heels and walked out.

We then had to appear before the German sergeant major who was quite a pleasant man but he had to go by the book and so he sentenced us to a further twelve days solitary confinement. For the first three days we had just bread and water and no bedding, no blankets, no mattress, then one day out of solitary and on normal rations, before reverting to another three days solitary on bread and water. I was so hungry, I wolfed the food straight away. It was those twelve days that were to seriously damage my health over the next forty years. I still have a card I wrote to my mum on the 21st October 1918, apologising for not having written earlier and really giving her the hint that I was unable to write because of certain difficulties.

FREDERICK HAMMOND

For those soldiers incapacitated by injury, like Fred, there was an alternative route out of Germany. Since 1915 a limited exchange of prisoners had taken place. However, in 1916, an alternative was agreed. Injured men would be sent into internment in Switzerland where they could receive better medical care than in POW camps. In May 1916, the first British prisoners were sent from Germany by train; by the Armistice nearly 27,000 former prisoners of all nationalities were residing there, including Fred.

I was exchanged because I was no good to them for doing any work with my hand. I was no use to them with the wounds I had and I could never fight again.

On the way to Switzerland the trains were crowded. Every time we stopped we used to get out and get boiling water from the engine and make some tea. I remember that we stopped at Frankfurt am Main where I caught the flu epidemic and I thought, 'Am I going to be able to get right through to Switzerland?' I hung on. I remember the camp at Frankfurt was between three ammunition factories, and the camp was there to protect them. We were there two or three days and our planes came over but did not drop any bombs. They used to come over and all the Germans would disappear and the prisoners would come out and cheer. And then we would cheer the Germans as they came out of the shelter. I had my 21st birthday there.

The flu was virulent at that time and soldiers were dying on the train. My head was throbbing but I wanted to get out of Germany and I wanted to live – get out and get home, that was my main thing, to get home again.

I don't remember the crossing into Switzerland but it was on the 22nd October 1918, and I remember the first night we stopped at Interlaken then the next day we went on to Wengen, Grindelwald, then up to Mürren with the hotel, the Hotel Belmont, at the top of the mountain. We overlooked the valley, the Jungfrau, the Mönch and the Eiger right in front of us. We were taken up into the bedroom, four to a room, where we had a lovely bed with a duvet, so thick, huge things they were, luxury down quilts. And we were waited on in the restaurant of the hotel, breakfast, mid-day meal and a meal at night. So different from Germany where we slept on a straw mattress and boards and big fleas to keep us company. We used to go walking every day, they had skating and five mile toboggan runs, all sorts of entertainment, football, cricket.

In Switzerland a dentist worked on my jaw and gradually I was able to open my mouth just a bit further. Every day he used to put an instrument between my teeth and gradually force them apart.

CHAPTER EIGHT

Release

Prisoners heard news of their impending release in a myriad ways. For those in France and Belgium, the final news came either from local villagers or, more often, through a German officer who merely stated that the war was over and that they were free to go. Not that the POWs hadn't had an inkling themselves, for they had been following an increasingly dishevelled German army for weeks. Now they were simply abandoned where they sat or lay, the Germans marching east with what they could carry while the British POWs, after picking themselves up, began their walk west, often passing along the same roads as retreating Germans.

For those in the camps, the announcement was no less perfunctory. Close to the French or Dutch borders, the news was wonderful but hardly unexpected, because here, too, information had been filtering through that the Germans were beaten. Only in the Kommandos, based miles away from parent camps, or in the hinterland of Germany, did the news of the Armistice come late or as a surprise. For a few working on isolated farms it never arrived at all.

By the terms of the Armistice, Germany was required to release all prisoners of war immediately and without reciprocity. This was fine in principle, but for the hundreds of thousands of Allied captives in the depths of Germany, there was nowhere to go. The POWs left in France or Belgium had the option of marching west to meet the advancing Allies. They were in friendly territory and most had little trouble in finding food and accommodation from liberated villagers only too happy to ply them with drink that they'd concealed for years and share what food they had. These POWs were quickly collected by the advance guard of Allied troops, the first two train loads of prisoners reaching the port of Calais only four days after the Armistice. But the POWs in Germany were not in the same position. Some who were held captive in the Rhineland did choose to make their own way back. However, as one group of POWs who entered Cologne found out, their presence was not welcomed by everyone and they were chased at knifepoint through the streets of the city, taking refuge in a hotel; this was an unusual but by no means isolated incident.

With Germany in a state of incipient revolution, many POWs awoke to find that the camp guards had merely packed up and gone, leaving them to roam the camps at will. More typically, an appeal was made through newspapers and by camp commandants for prisoners to stay where they were until adequate transport was made available to take them away. The process of repatriation was slow and cumbersome, not least because it suited the Germans to slow down the traffic of prisoners to the west, using them as bargaining chips to delay or mitigate other Allied demands. Despite protests and threats by the British, the Germans claimed that such were the requirements for railway engines and rolling stock by the Allies, that there were simply not enough trains to collect prisoners. Of 88 ambulance trains, only eight were serviceable according to German reports. It all meant that when trains were provided, some prisoners were transported without proper medical supervision, including one train that arrived in Cologne with 512 prisoners on board of whom no fewer than 33 were found to be dead.

By the end of November, fewer than ten per cent of POWs had reached England, and by the middle of December only half of all POWs had reached Allied lines. For many prisoners, there was no option but to suffer what felt like an interminable wait in POW camps across Germany. Even by the beginning of January 1919, two months after the end of the war, at least 14,000 British POWs were still languishing in Germany. This was a British estimate; as no consolidated nominal roll was kept by the Germans the only way to find out precisely was to despatch Red Cross units to all 21 Army Corps Districts in Germany to locate, and arrange the return of, missing POWs. It was not until late January and early February that most of the remaining prisoners were able to obtain safe passage home.

The POWs returned on a multitude of boats from Calais, Boulogne and Rotterdam, but also from the ports of Hamburg and Copenhagen. Many, too weak to make the journey, were kept behind in Allied camps to recuperate and put on a bit of weight before going home. When they did return, they docked at one of three ports, Dover, Hull or Leith, before being sent to dispersal camps such as those at Ripon and Canterbury. It was here that many were questioned for the first time about their treatment in Germany. Statements were made and taken down for future use in the prosecution of war criminals, and disabilities assessed. However, most prisoners were not interested. More than anything, they wanted to get home and take advantage of a two-month prisoner of war leave, sensibly granted by the Government.

ERNIE STEVENS

One evening, we were coming back from the factory and we passed the night shift who were going on, and they told us the war was over. What a relief, knowing that it would not be long before we would be home, thankful that I had got to the end of this horrible experience – and it was a horrible experience.

We went to work the next day, but the second day we decided that was it, and we demanded that the Germans unlock the gates to let us walk freely into the town. The Board of the factory actually gave us a fifty-mark note to spend, as

The darker side of captivity. A secret picture taken of two prisoners tied to a post as punishment at Soltau Camp. It is not known how this image was taken. However, one POW at another camp later recalled how a Frenchman had frequently carried a crucifix though the camp, in what appeared to be religious zeal. Unbeknown to the Germans, the base of the crucifix held a hidden camera.

Men of various nationalities pose for the camera, along with their assorted pots and pans. These were commonly used on makeshift fires built to brew up or cook any extra food that men had been sent or which they had managed to scrounge.

Just one a large number of British POWs who nearly starved to death in German captivity.

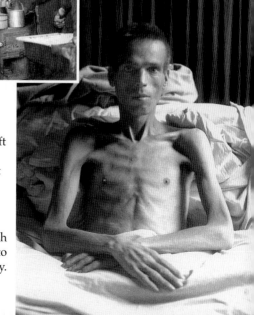

Hauspital Cemetery as it appeared during the war. Postwar, almost all British graves in Germany were collected and taken to one of four permanent war cemeteries in Cologne, Berlin, Kassel, and Hamburg.

Arthur Smith's and Jacob Martin's graves as they were in Münster I (Hauspital Cemetery). Both were later reinterred in Cologne's Southern Cemetery.

January 2000, Hauspital Cemetery as it appears today.

A postcard showing the original French design of the memorial.

POUR NOS MORTS

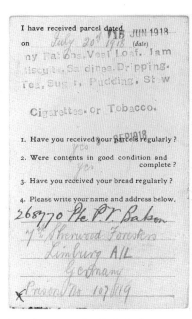

A card returned to Britain by a POW from Jack Rogers' battalion confirming that his food parcels are reaching him satisfactorily.

Members of the Red Cross visiting Freidrichsfeld Camp.

Red cross parcels for the two hundred British prisoners held at Guben Camp, Brandenburg.

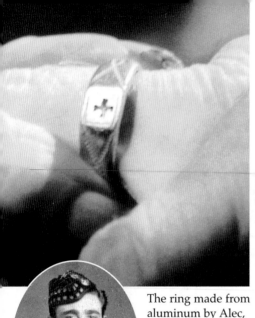

The ring made from aluminum by Alec, a Russian POW, and given to Tommy Gay. Tommy wore the ring for over 82 years, until he died in 1999.

Ernie Stevens (top) with other prisoners including Sid Stillwell, with whom he escaped from the soda factory in early October 1918.

The soda factory at Rheinberg. The heaps of coal, the wall that Ernie and Sid climbed over and the road which they crossed, can all clearly be seen in the picture.

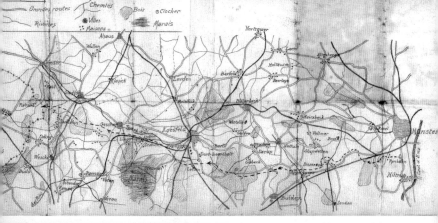

A map actually carried by an escapee from Münster II (Rennbahn) POW Camp. The route of his attempted get-away to Holland can be clearly seen. Like Ernie Stevens, the escapee was captured on the border, but somehow managed to hide the map to keep as a souvenir.

A soldier of the West Yorkshire Regiment in uniform and as he appeared after his successful escape from Germany back to England.

Part of a brief diary written by Ernie Stevens when he records the presence of the Crown Prince on the same train.

After his release from solitary confinement, Ernie Stevens wrote this card home to his mother, hinting that something unusual had happened.

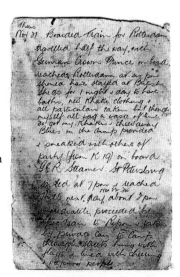

A hurriedly taken snapshot of the Kaiser standing at a station in Holland. A similar scene greeted Ernie Stevens at Rhurmond station when he witnessed the Kaiser's son following his father into exile.   IWM Q47933

Kassel Camp, January 1919. A British soldier sent to find missing POWs watches as records are checked for prisoners who remain unaccounted for..

Ernie Stevens with his mother and half-sister, Gladys. On his return from Germany, Ernie was heartbroken to find that Gladys had just died from the great flu epidemic that swept Europe in 1918.

Jack Rogers' mother was relieved at seeing her son home again after four years of war service.

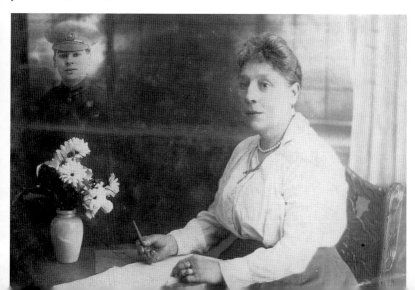

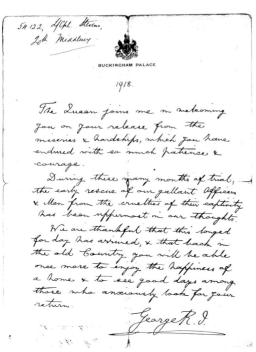

The letter sent to Ernie Stevens and all other POWs on their return from France. Although duplicated en-masse, this personal letter was much appreciated by almost all of the former prisoners.

Arthur Hoyland (far right, standing) at Schneidemühl Camp. It was after his stay at Münster that his troubles really began.

(Below left) A postwar picture of Arthur Hoyland as he appeared in his passport.

(Below) The stamp which appears on Arthur Hoyland's passport giving him permission to enter Germany to give evidence at the Leipzig Trials in May 1921. He left the country for home again just five days later.

DESCRIPTION OF BEARER.

PHOTOGRAPH OF BEARER.

SIGNATURE OF BEARER.

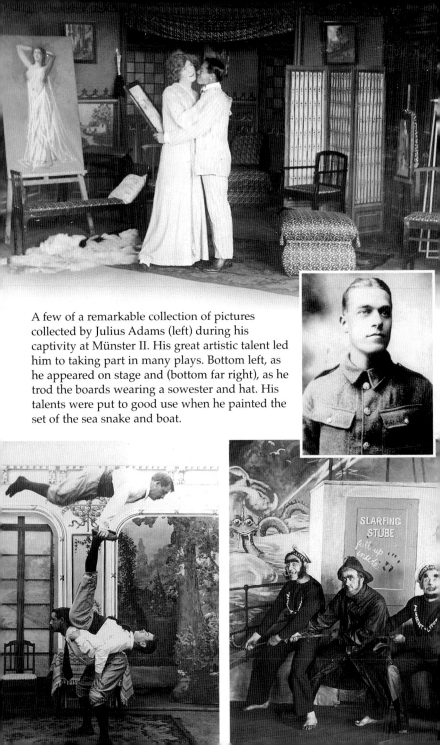

A few of a remarkable collection of pictures collected by Julius Adams (left) during his captivity at Münster II. His great artistic talent led him to taking part in many plays. Bottom left, as he appeared on stage and (bottom far right), as he trod the boards wearing a sowester and hat. His talents were put to good use when he painted the set of the sea snake and boat.

Some of the artwork that Julius Adams drew while a POW. The picture of Julius Adams drawing was painted by an admiring French POW. Note the clogs that most POWs wore at some time during captivity.

Alfred Schofield as a POW aged 34, and his death certificate four years later, when, unable to live with the memories of war, he committed suicide under a train.

Registration District. *Easthampstead*

1922. Death in the Sub-district of *Bracknell* in the County of *Berks*

No.	When and where Died.	Name and Surname.	Sex.	Age.	Rank or Profession.	Cause of Death.	Signature, Description and Residence of Informant.	When Registered.	Signature of Registrar.
1.	Twenty third February 1922 London & South Western Railway line near Swinley Bridge Winkfield No. 29.	Alfred Henry Schofield	Male	37 years	of 36 Linden Road Stamford Hill London a Fishmongers manager	Killed by train on the L. & S.W. while trespassing	Certificate received from Robert 3 Payne Coroner for Berks. Reading District Inquest held 25 February 1922	Twenty Seventh February 1922	E. Wright Registrar.

I, *Edwin L. Wright* Registrar of Births and Deaths for the Sub-district of *Bracknell*, in the County of *Berks* do hereby certify that this is a true Copy of the Entry No. *1*, in the Register Book of Deaths for the said Sub-district, and that such Register Book is now legally in my custody.

WITNESS MY HAND this *11th* day of *March*, 1922.

E. Wright

Registrar of Births and Deaths.

our POW pay had no value outside the camp. I guess it was to encourage us to go back to work, but we didn't. I know that I went into town and had a good meal and then bought some postcards, including one of the soda factory where I'd worked. The Germans we met were very quiet, and looked crestfallen. As we walked along, two or three of us together, they got off the pavement and walked in the gutter. It was gentlemanly, shall we say, but personally I didn't believe in that sort of thing. It was another week after the Armistice that we were told to get ready to board a train at Rheinberg station, which would take us to the border. The train could not pass over the border into Holland so we got out, walked over the frontier and were taken, by private cars, to Roermond, a military post in the south of Holland. There some of us stayed in a farmer's hayloft for the night and in the morning we woke, had breakfast and were taken to catch a train for Rotterdam.

At Roermond station we were told to wait at the rear of a train, just forty of us, when an officer of the Dutch army who spoke excellent English came up and called us to attention. He told us to be quiet and to listen carefully, as very soon a number of high ranking German officers would be coming on to the platform towards the far end of the train and that on no account were we to make any noise whatsoever. We mustn't whistle, mustn't sing, shout, comment, nothing. After a few minutes we saw some German officers looking like Christmas trees, all plastered with colours and shiny boots. Then almost at the end of the group came a guy I'd seen caricatures of in various magazines and papers in Britain. It was Crown Prince Wilhelm, the Crown Prince of Germany. Ugly looking guy, terrible looking, had a nose that stuck out probably a foot in front of his face, to see him in person made me almost sick. He was tall, he must have been at least six foot, making him stand out from the big nobs that were surrounding him. They weren't interested in us at all. The Prince, or 'Little Willie' as he was known, was going into exile in Holland like his father shortly before. And all this crowd -travelled on the same train as ourselves, although I never saw them get off.

GEORGE GADSBY

We arrived at Fleurus and made preparations to stay the night outside the town in some open sheds. In the morning, after a terribly cold night, they placed us in a factory with other prisoners to await further orders. Early in the evening, some Belgians rushed up the stairs with some hot soup and we were surprised to find them wearing English and Belgian ribbons. They told us the war was over and needless to say, we shook the dust off the ceiling with cheering. We managed to get a good stock of wood and round a bright fire we enjoyed a happy evening, singing.

The next morning, the Germans took us to Namur where we were escorted to a small church on the outskirts. During the evening, the Germans raided a barge containing wine, bringing several cases into the church. All the Germans were drunk, and some threatened to throw their Sergeant major into the canal on the opposite side of the road. Several broken bottles lay on the church floor and the stench of wine was awful.

Early the following morning, the Germans wanted us to renew our journey to Cologne but we knew the terms of the Armistice and refused to go any further. At the first opportunity we all left the church and went on our own, the Germans eventually leaving us, pulling their own carts.

We stayed in Namur with Belgian friends, enjoying the pleasure of watching the defeated German Army retire. A donkey and a calf shared the pulling of one wagon, the wounded were launched on the top of heavily laden wagons, men were cursing, and all the German soldiers wore strands of red ribbon proclaiming revolution against the Kaiser. Some of them, as they came out of the estaminets drunk, were singing the 'Marseillaise'. The Germans raided several stores and barges, most of them containing wine and spirits.

About a dozen wagons of large calibre shells and a wagon of cordite were left by the Germans in a small siding. As we were walking on the riverside, we noticed that one of the wagons was on fire. A Belgian had fixed his horse to the opposite end of the wagons and endeavoured to pull them away from the burning one. We hastened to help, but we had not gone five yards when a shell burst and shrapnel fell quite near us. The Belgian loosed the horse and we sought shelter in a cave in the rock which surrounds Namur. Here, fortunately, houses intervened and prevented the shrapnel from causing direct hits at our place of safety. We were imprisoned for three hours before the explosions subsided. We then retreated as fast as we could from the burning wagons, suffering from a headache caused by the vibration. Several houses were demolished and two children killed. It was supposed that the wagon of cordite had been ignited by children playing with loose bits lying about and then the conflagration spread to the wagons containing the shells.

After about a week, our troops, arrayed in new khaki, arrived in the city. The clashing steel, the roll of the gun carriages, the martial airs, the long ranks of soldiers and the Lancers with their pennants fluttering in the breeze, formed a striking contrast to the ragged, dirty columns of Germans that had so recently passed through the city.

JACK ROGERS

When addressing them, the commandant had always referred to the prisoners of Münster I as 'Schweinehunde'. On Armistice morning, however, the tone changed.

One particular morning, we were all brought out on parade and the commandant spoke to his interpreter and the first

155

word this little man said was 'Gentlemen'. You can just imagine the roar that went up when he said that, cheering, shouting, he couldn't keep us quiet. After a bit everything settled and he said the war was over for us. All we had to do was to wait until they could bring a train and evacuate us. In the meantime, would we be patient and stop where we were, to keep the camp going until the necessary arrangements could be made.

At Münster railway station, there had accumulated hundreds of small Red Cross parcels, almost like a brick wall, parcels which were supposed to have been delivered to the prisoners. They were no good to us but we were still extremely cross and we did not want German soldiers to have them. So we had a chat amongst ourselves and said that if the authorities could arrange for all the poor people in the village to come to the station, we prisoners would be there to hand them each a parcel. We knew they'd had very little food and they'd had a rough time, believe me, so wouldn't it be a grand gesture before we went? The next day there were queues of people all lined up, waiting, and we all had the privilege of giving a parcel and you ought to have seen them, the looks on their faces.

To be going home, it was marvellous. I thought, what's it going to be like – just to see my people again, you know, to be free, oh, I couldn't believe it.

We got in a train and went over the border into Holland to a little place called Enschede. We arrived in late afternoon and they welcomed us with open arms. They'd got this village hall and they had borrowed all sorts of mattresses and as we lay there, the local people came in and they brought all sorts of goods to eat and drink. We didn't undress, we just lay there and slept.

The next day we went down to Rotterdam where we were to pick up our ship to take us across to England. When we got down there, a heavy fog had descended on the port, so much so that the Captain of the ship said he couldn't sail as it was too dangerous. A train took us back to Enschede but instead of going into the village hall we were taken to a place called Timbertown. This little town was made by British Marines who'd escaped capture in October 1914 by going to Holland where they had been interned for the duration of the war. The Marines had now gone home except one naval officer who stayed behind to give us some advice. He told us we were going home with what he hoped was a clean bill of health, but he'd like to warn us of two particular things. One, he said, was to avoid the Schnapps, which he said were very dangerous, and the other was to avoid the women. 'I can assure you that you have got to watch out for them very carefully,' he told us earnestly. He needn't have worried because we hadn't any money anyway.

PERCY WILLIAMS

By November I was in a little hospital in Bremen. I had gone down from twelve to six or seven stone, my leg was giving me trouble, and my head was covered in sores from malnutrition. I was cold and I was hungry and my one thought was how much longer was this going to last. I was desperate to get away, to get home.

One night I heard some noise, it sounded like rifle firing and I asked a German guard what was going on but was told it was nothing, 'nichts, nichts'. It wasn't until three or four days later that a doctor was coming round and I noticed he was no longer in his army uniform but in civilian clothes. I asked him and he said, 'There's an Armistice, but it's only for a few days, it'll start again, you'll see.' We didn't know anything else for a fortnight because we were so isolated. We had no newspapers and there was no radio in those days, so I was sent under armed guard back to Bremerhaven and carried on working for a few more days before we were told that we weren't to work any more, the war was over.

157

We couldn't believe our luck that after all this time the war had finished and we should go back to England. But so many of the men were ill, a lot of them were dying from the influenza epidemic. The clothes used to hang off them and their faces were thin. Their arms were thin, their legs were thin, they were not in a position to work, they could hardly stand, some of them. There were men of all nationalities in the camp – French, Belgians, there were some Russians, great big fellows who were now all skin and bones, scores and scores died and we had to dig the graves. In Bremen there was an Australian called Wheatley, he was a big chap, six footer, an engine driver from Sydney, and he was in the next bed to mine. One day I asked the German orderly where Wheatley was and he said he was 'kaput, kaput'. He'd died and they'd buried him already. That upset me terribly. He'd been a prisoner for a couple of years and was as thin as a rake, he'd lost all his colour, coughing all the time. In the end he couldn't breath. He looked desperately ill – no resistance.

After the Armistice we were sent to Parchim camp, a huge camp of perhaps 10,000 prisoners. We were there about a month, and scores and scores of men died there, mainly Russians, who'd been imprisoned for three or four years. I know because I was picked to dig many of the graves in the camp's sandy soil. From there I was sent to Helsingborg in Sweden, where we recuperated and were properly fed before we sailed to Leith, where I was able to send a telegram home saying that I was alive. I then moved to hospital in Ripon where my parents came up to visit. They were delighted to see me because there were so many people from Llandrindod and from Pembroke who had died and here I was, with only just a bit of trouble with my leg.

TOMMY GAY

We didn't hear about the war ending for some five or six weeks afterwards. We didn't know the war was over until one morning we were told we'd all got to be out on parade because one of our captains was coming to take charge at 9am the following morning. We were all out there, of course, lined up, and sure enough at 9 o'clock in came the captain and we all stood to attention – 'Morning sir,' you know – and then he told us. 'The war is finished and the Germans are no longer in control, I am in charge of you boys now. The gates are going to be opened in the morning and you will be free to go out and enjoy life again. Stroll around, have a pint if you have the money, go where you want within a one mile radius, but no further. Don't go trying to run home because it won't work, one mile radius and that's all.' So of course with that away he went. We were excited at the thought that we could go and enjoy ourselves with the few coppers we had in our pockets. While we were working we were paid three pieces of metal a day, it wasn't really money, but we could spend it at a little shop in the camp and buy a postcard or a letter. We spent the day imagining what it would be like when we saw a pub and were served with a pint. That would be freedom, absolute freedom.

Two men were so excited that the war was finished that they were going out of the camp, they were not willing to wait until the morning. They tried to jump over the top and they killed themselves. They were electrocuted; the Germans hadn't switched the wire off. Mad, just excitement knowing that the war was finished and they would soon be going home, but they never went home. The rest of the lads said to each other that they must have been bleedin' crazy, couldn't wait five minutes. I didn't know it was electrified, nor did anybody else that I know of. We had no idea, all we knew was that outside there were sentries walking up and down, every few yards.

FRANK DEANE

A Frenchman told us there had been an Armistice, a day or two after it had happened. We knew there was likely to be one as this man could speak German and he used to get the news and he'd translate it into French and he'd tell us. It wasn't very easy for me – my French wasn't very good - but I managed to discover that things were going very well. About a week after the Armistice we were brought back into Kassel, into the camp proper, and we were told to wait there until we were fetched. The British Government didn't want all the prisoners of war trekking to the frontiers so they issued an order to stay put, which was sensible. We waited there until just after Christmas, in fact I had Christmas dinner in the camp, eating a little tin of cold mutton from one of the parcels. It was rather tiresome waiting, but then you got used to waiting in the army, waiting, waiting, waiting, always bloody well waiting. We received no more food parcels because of the fire in the parcel shop, so we had to return to living on the muck the Germans gave us, so the last month of capture ended up rather like the first. On New Year's Eve, a beautiful Red Cross train drew up in Kassel station and we were just told to get in it. It was so nice to see such a nice comfortable Red Cross train with nice comfortable Red Cross nurses and we thought, 'Oh, we are in clover now', but it was only until we got to Cologne. We arrived about 5pm and they turned us out in the city for a few hours, just to look around. I remember the bridge and I remember some British Grenadiers standing guard in front of a building there and I thought how smart they looked. Later that evening we were gathered together to board cattle trucks for the rest of the two day journey to Calais.

NORMAN COWAN

Although I had a bandage on my hand, my palm had repaired sufficiently for me to be classed fit to go back to work. About 20 of us paraded to go back to the salt mines, but by this time we'd heard through the French that they were expecting the Armistice to be signed and that widespread revolts were breaking out all over Germany. All we knew was that no more work was to be done outside the camp, so although we paraded as requested, we refused to go to the mines. We stood there in front of this very violent NCO who ordered us to go, but we had an interpreter who told him that the war was finished. 'The Armistice has been signed, there's no more battle, so we're not going out, we're not going into the salt mines.' He became furious and used words in German and French, which we didn't understand, but we stuck to our guns. He walked about waving his sabre, but eventually had to give in and went to the commandant. That day we stood there for about three hours in the biting winter cold before the commandant came and read a notice saying that as long as we looked after our latrines and the amenities of the camp, we could stay. We were very boisterous and returned to our billets congratulating ourselves on having won.

On 12th of November, the commandant confirmed that the Armistice had been signed but that no details of our possible departure were available. Thoughts of a return soon to Blighty were much in evidence and our senior NCOs' committee, who had lain low in their private quarters, now came to the surface and discussed ways and means to get us into some order for what they said would be our soon departure. Only in the Russian compound was there real despair. They had no representation to plead their cause and really nowhere to go. The Russian revolution was causing great chaos which would continue for years, so the troops languished in these German prison camps without hope and without extra food, existing only on POW rations meagrely provided by their captors.

Our hope that we would soon be on our way was quickly dispelled, as news came through that a general order had been issued that no further returning POWs were to pass through advancing British troops in the west. Apparently the sight of starving POWs working on light railways behind the German lines had dismayed and greatly angered British troops on their way to occupy Germany and retaliation was feared. We would leave Germany via a port in the Baltic but in the meantime we had to wait for the repatriating officers to come. Our senior committee tried to organise games and entertainment with some success while we waited, but days turned into weeks before news came that these officers were on their way to Quedlinburg camp, by which time we felt almost entirely forgotten.

When the officers came, there was a mass meeting in the compound where we were promised that any injustices by the Germans would be severely dealt with by our High Command. The men had heard such promises before and were more interested in the food stores which they brought with them. Soon after, they stripped us of anything in the nature of shirts and gave us something else to wear, to help get rid of the lice. The taste of a brew of real tea with carnation milk and sugar and also the taste of old plum or apple jam was lovely. They also came with parcels of biscuits, each biscuit the size of a hand. They told us to bore holes into the underside of the biscuits, soak them in water and put them on a shelf and in the morning they would have swollen into a bread bun-like consistency. However, the rats knew better and we found they had eaten the biscuits by the morning, so from then on we learned to keep them in bed beside us.

After some days, German lorries came to transport us to Quedlinburg Station to board converted cattle trucks. These took us the long journey north to Stettin on the Baltic, where we were met at the port by the King of Denmark's yacht which King Haakon had converted into a hospital ship with Danish Red Cross nurses. I was on a stretcher for, although my leg muscle and bone were gradually healing, the scar on the back thigh muscle continued to suppurate, and I suffered from severe cramp. On the boat, we crossed the straits to Copenhagen in Denmark where we stayed for several months for rest and rehabilitation, for many men were not fit to meet the world after the difficulties of living in restricted conditions on meagre rations. After weeks recuperating and fattening up, we left, one very wet and windy morning, on a converted cargo ship called the *Ajax* and set sail for Leith in Scotland. Having been so well fed in Denmark, some men began to complain about the quality of food on board ship. A rather annoyed chef made an announcement that he was prepared to give a gold sovereign to anyone who ate the dinner provided on the *Ajax* when the ship entered the North Sea the next day. A big storm blew up and the rocking and tossing of the ship gave all but the crew a severe bout of seasickness, myself included. We all spent most of the journey hanging onto the sides of the rigging and being truly ill.

WALTER HUMPHRYS

The day before the Armistice, we were passing through Charleroi and a lot of the local people seemed to be very excited, a few flags were waved. But we didn't think much of it, we thought they'd just had good news. As the Germans retired, we preceded them, sleeping anywhere, anyhow, sometimes by the side of the road, sometimes on the floor of a building, we had no option. I had a breaking out on my right leg, my calf, and that night we stopped outside a German Red Cross station and I walked into this place and I showed this sanitary sergeant doctor my leg and he pointed to a stool. I put my foot up and he walked across to his bench, picked up a lance and came along and squashed it and just pointed to the door, nothing on it and I walked out with it all dripping out of my calf. He was pretty cruel.

We were near Namur the day the Armistice was signed and were told to celebrate the occasion although we had no food of any sort, there being no rations. Most of the Germans got drunk, the camp cook being violently struck by a sentry for no reason whatsoever. We continued to march with the Germans and it wasn't until three days later that we were released. We were in a farm overnight without food or water, then late in the afternoon a German officer walked into the yard and said, 'As the Armistice has been signed, you can do as you like as we have no food for you. You are free. We are going back to Germany.' And he walked out and left us there. Everybody scrabbled out to make sure they were free, where they intended to go when it was nearly dark I don't know. Four of us who were great mates decided there was no point going anywhere that night so we climbed up into a barn and got a good night's rest, sleeping on the hay. We got up early in the morning, left the farmyard and set off to find our troops, retracing our steps. Very soon we began passing columns of Germans marching on the other side of the road, going back towards Germany, some were glad, others frowned.

The first place we came to was an estaminet, in the evening, and the owner gave us something to drink and some potatoes and said we could sleep on the floor. Next morning off we went again and got to Charleroi. We were looking in a window when two girls came up and said if we went back to their houses we would get some food, so two went with one and two with the other, they were neighbours. We continued walking, and although I was very thin, I weighed no more than seven stone, I was still strong because while I had always been on the slim side, I had been quite muscular. We walked until we met our own troops and I was sent to hospital in Mons with my leg still suppurating.

BILL EASTON

In the last weeks of the war, Bill had been working at a hotel in
Friedrichsfeld, laying a new dance hall floor. Leni Mörrs had
been his supervisor.

I went to work as usual one morning, and Leni, she came
up and kissed me. It was the first time she showed any
emotion and she said that the Kaiser had gone to Holland and
that there was an Armistice. I nearly had a fit. I asked her if
she was sure and she said 'Yes' so I went back to the camp
and, of course, immediately there was trouble. Those people
who'd been -prisoners for a long time, they wanted to break
out straight away, they were hotheads.

By the time the Red Cross came, I was working as an
orderly on a ward, about fifteen of us altogether. We were told
that an evacuation hospital was being set up and would we
wait where we were for one or two weeks. So we agreed to
stop but we never heard any more, not a soul came to see us
after then, the British army, the Red Cross, no one. No further
parcels came, so after two weeks one of the chaps said, 'I'm
fed up with this, I'm going to Holland in the morning.' We
tried to stop him but he'd found out there was a train that
used to go up from Germany and along the frontier, so in the
end we had a majority vote and we decided that we'd all go.

We got on this train, no one said a word to us, and went
into Holland and headed for Nijmegen, ten or twelve miles
away. We got to this place called Zeevenar, and the villagers
treated us very nicely and we stopped the night in the schoolroom. They fed us in the morning and a squad of soldiers
came to take us to the fortress at Nijmegen.

From Nijmegen we were sent one afternoon down to the
docks at Rotterdam. We all had a good bath and we changed
uniform and they took us onto an American luxury liner, two
to a cabin, with private bathrooms. I went to sleep. It was
early evening when the bugle went, fall in, and we all had to

scramble upstairs. There were a lot of men on deck and we fell in, to be marched straight off the boat only to watch this liner pull away, goodness knows where to. Any rate, they said we were for the SS something or other, a cargo boat headed for England, and because it was mild we would be sleeping out on the deck. Presently, a file of armed soldiers came on and we thought they were guards for us but they were to protect the boat against mines in the sea. Afterwards we lined the side of the boat and we could see these mines bobbing like bottles in the sea, although I never saw one blown up.

The next place we saw were the lights of Yarmouth. We anchored off the town for the night and cases of Bass beer were sent out to the boat, of which we were allowed one each. We slept out again and the next morning we were damned hungry, for which we were given just biscuits and tea, then off we sailed for Hull.

THOMAS SPRIGGS

Repatriation came relatively quickly for prisoners in France or near Germany's western border. Thomas Spriggs had been in a German camp but had been sent back to labour near the front line. He was one of the lucky prisoners to return home before the end of November 1918, although his arrival at his parents' house was totally unexpected.

On 11th November 1918 at 11 o'clock in the morning, one of the postens came along, opened the gates and said, 'Off you go, clear off.' That was the first we knew the war was over and we didn't wait a minute before we were on our way. That first day about 30 of us made our way back to a place called Enghien, on the field of the battle of Waterloo. We slept that night in a schoolroom and the next day we made our way further on towards Mons, but before we got there we met up with the Canadian Army, and they fed us and took us on to the town. We stayed there for a couple of days, then went on to Arras, where we were put on an empty wagon train which took us to Calais. We took a boat to Dover and we arrived on November 30th 1918, 12 months to the day since I'd been captured.

I remember the vessel hooting, and the ships in the harbour, their sirens were going to give us a good welcome into Dover, their crews cheering. Oh, I was very happy to set foot in England again, very pleased to think I was back. We went by special train to London but by the time we reached St Pancras, it was too late to set off to the little village in Leicestershire where my family was. I'd got some old friends at St Alwyns and I stayed with them overnight and went the next day to John of Gaunt Station it was called in those days – closed now – and who should get off the train at the same time but my eldest brother who had come home on leave from France. He was in the Army Service Corps, so we both walked in the door together. I don't know if my mother was expecting my brother but she certainly wasn't expecting me. We weren't a very demonstrative family, my mother especially. She was pleased to see me, no doubt about that, but it was a question of 'How are you?' 'How are you getting on?' It didn't make me sad, because my family was never like that, falling around each other's necks. Freedom after being a prisoner, you can't quite realise what it's like.

ERNIE STEVENS

At Rotterdam, we were told that we would be getting on a boat the next day. This meant that we were to go into one of the warehouses and sleep, but I said to Sid, 'We don't want to wait until the morning, come on, let's go and join this crowd lining up to get on the boat.' This we did, and we crossed over that night and landed at Hull, where we took a special train to Ripon Camp in Yorkshire.

There were crowds of people on both sides of the Humber, waving and shouting out 'Welcome back', hundreds waving all kinds of handkerchiefs and Union Jacks. We had lined the sides of the boat and we were waving back and it was great to feel that you were welcomed home in such a way, a real eye-opener. And when we got on the train to go to Ripon Camp there were people on both sides of the track all the way. I haven't the slightest doubt that they had been told that a special train was coming through, containing prisoners of war. You've got to remember that our camp was very close to Holland, so we were one of the very first groups to be brought out of Germany, that this was less than two weeks after the Armistice. It was great to be on British soil again but equally there were so many pent up feelings and emotions too. It was very difficult to hold yourself in check.

JACK ROGERS

Owing to thick fog, Jack had not been able to cross the North Sea to England and had been sent to stay, temporarily, in a former internment camp.

We were at Timbertown for about three days and nights before we travelled home via Rotterdam to Hull, on a ship called the *Kronstadt*. No sooner had we sailed out into the North Sea than the fog descended again and, as there were still floating mines about, the Captain stopped the ship and anchored for the night. In the morning the fog lifted and with the boat full of steam, off we went. Later, as we sailed up the Humber into Hull, all the sirens of the ships were sounded, bells were ringing, bangers going off and hooters blowing. There were great crowds of people, as we were the first prisoners to arrive there, about 150 of us in all. There was a long train waiting for us. We climbed aboard, and as we looked out of the carriage windows, up and down the platform were any amount of women. These poor mothers were walking up and down the platform, each of them carrying a picture of a missing son or husband. They came up and showed you the picture and asked, 'Did you know him? Have you seen him? Was he in your regiment?' And so forth, all up and down the train. You wanted to give them a little hope, to say we had seen them, but no, we hadn't, we couldn't tell them anything. Finally, we were taken off to the repatriation centre at Ripon in Yorkshire. Before we were allowed to go home, we had to drop everything and have a series of showers to make sure you did not take home any disease or any lice, that sort of thing. Each man was given a big towel to put round him, then we walked through a big hall and all along the walls were different people with different clothing to hand out: vests, shirts, socks, shoes, then either a new uniform or suit. After this, we had to see a series of doctors and they were asking us to tell them of anything that we'd suffered or were suffering in any way resulting from the war or being a -prisoner. They were going to make the Germans pay for every penny of it, or so they said. That was for the powers that be, the Government to decide. But you must remember the Germans hadn't got much left themselves to pay with, so what they were going to do, I don't know. Unfortunately for me, I'd lost the use completely of my right ear. I'd done a lot of shooting as a sniper all through the war and I'd been banging away until my whole hearing from my right ear went. I thought, as I went through this series of doctors asking me this, asking me that, should I tell them I'd lost the use of my right ear or should I wait until I got home? I'd not been home for four years and I thought that, being a young man, maybe my hearing might come back again, so I decided to wait. I didn't say anything and they passed me through. However, the hearing never came back, so I've had to make do all my life with just my left ear.

FRANK DEANE

It was a very stormy weekend and the boats weren't sailing that day, so we had to go into camp at Calais, a tented camp on the sands, until the next day when we sailed to Dover in rough seas. We landed at the quayside where we entrained directly and were sent to Canterbury for two days, where we were rigged out in our proper uniform. Soon after, I took a train to Liverpool, arriving in the afternoon when my father, who'd taken an hour off work, met me at Lyme Street station. I don't remember it being a very emotional moment. I'm not a very emotional person in that way, none of the weeping or anything of that sort. There were no crowds waving us home, it was New Year by then and coming home was a staid business, there was nothing to celebrate. Then again, what recognition would you expect? I just wanted some food, a bath and a bed.

NORMAN COWAN

We berthed in the darkness at Leith and were taken to some barracks, where the next day we assembled to be welcomed home and to be told again by the officer in command that they were going to bring the Germans to account for the condition of our men. We said between ourselves, 'I hope that's true', but we knew it wouldn't be, and that's the way it happened. They said, 'Leave it to us, we're going to see that what is wrong is put right with the prisoners of war.' And we said in our minds 'That will be the day' and it worked out that way. Our desire was to be free and see our families and friends again.

A few days later, we received new uniforms, pay books and identity documents and were assigned to train groups to take us back to our regimental depots. Many farewells were expressed to pals from other regiments who had been with us through the POW days, before a train came to take us away. From Leith, they took us on the East Coast route, invariably passing through Newcastle, so I thought, 'I'll drop off at Newcastle and go back home.' Not on your life, the train didn't even stop, it choo-chooed through and I was taken down to Tidworth, on Salisbury Plain, the depot where I'd been trained on the Hotchkiss Gun two years before. There was a sergeant there, with whom I got friendly, and he told me that only those in gainful employment were going to be given leave. He said, 'Now, you'll never get leave telling them you're just ordinary, why don't you become a driller?' I said, 'I've never drilled soldiers in my life before,' and he said, 'I'm not talking about drills in the army. Major Stevens who looks after discharges is going away for about a fortnight. Captain Brummell, belonging to your old regiment, is taking over. When he comes, tell him you're a driller.' I said, 'He'll know' – 'He won't know'. I went before Captain Brummell and he asked my occupation so I said 'driller'. 'What sort?' he asked, and I told him I drilled holes in steel before I joined up and it got me my leave. I was given prisoner of war leave for three months so soldiers like me could get our jobs back. But people like me who'd been licking stamps at sixteen years and three months were just nothing.

BILL EASTON

We arrived at Hull, but they told us they didn't want us there but further up the River Humber. By the time we drew up to a quay, we were fed up to the teeth. There was a rail that ran right along the quay and all along the back of this railway there were tea tables all laid out and some old general came on board with a cocked hat and made a speech, 'Welcome home' and all this, that, and the other; we weren't interested. They told us we could eat what we liked within reason, then they dropped the chains near the gangway and we made a

171

dash for the food. We'd only just got to these tables when a passenger train pulled up and they said, 'Sorry, things have altered, we can't stop this train here as it is booked later in the day and it must go now. You'll get a reception at the other end.' Well, we had to board and we were damned hungry and swearing, because the lads had had hardly any time to grab some food.

We were taken to a place four miles from Ripon and shown into huts. There was a lot of argument about this because these huts formed part of a prison camp and we were alongside prisoners from the *Emden*, the cruiser that was sunk in the war, and these fellows were sauntering around like they were on parole, dressed up to the nines. The lads were furious.

We were dog-tired and went and had a sleep. In the morning a bugle went, someone got up and looked. It was about 7 o'clock in the morning, I should think, and we got the order to turn out. The Germans were having urns of tea taken into their huts when a sergeant came into our barracks and said, 'Come on, fall in.' The things they called him. He said, 'Come on, you are still in the army.' 'Oh, bugger off,' they were saying to him, and we refused to get up. A colonel was sent for and he came in and at first he cajoled us, 'Come on, lads, don't spoil the record.' But they said the same to him. He started to get angry then, saying he could place us in close confinement, as some of our lads were threatening to attack these Germans. We then demanded a cup of tea, which was brought, after which we were ordered out on parade again. One fellow, a Yorkshireman, he said that we were not for turning out, 'We've had enough of that', and 'It was a damn sight worse than being prisoners.' The colonel said we could be charged with mutiny, but of course that didn't happen. We weren't allowed out of the hut after that.

The colonel had had enough. He wanted rid of us and told us he would apply to headquarters to see if the necessary paperwork could be rushed through to clear us out and give us our two months' POW leave. We were given a very poor breakfast and by dinnertime, well, we didn't get any dinner, they'd signed the lot of us off.

We were taken down to the station and we had to go to York, where I caught the Midland Great Northern down to Peterborough, then changing to the Great Eastern for Kings Lynn. It seemed like I would never get there. Eventually, I caught the midnight mail train and turned up on the doorstep about 3am and of course my parents nearly had a fit. They made a real fuss of me, of course.

CHAPTER NINE

Coming home

The first prisoners of war who came home were fêted, if not as conquerors, then at least as the lads who had stoically survived imprisonment. Civilians lined river-banks, packed railway stations and skirted the pavements to welcome the boys home. They were caught up in an imme-diate post-war euphoria, when few other troops were readily available to be cheered and clapped. The excitement was to fade quickly. Within weeks, the image of returning soldiers became so normal that by the time the last significant batch of prisoners came home in late January 1919 there was really no one to be seen, no one to hail their return.

Most civilians and soldiers were never to see the shocking state in which some prisoners returned, although official photographs of a few survive in the archives. Those who did come across the prisoners were appalled by what they saw, one writing that even though he had served three years on the Western Front, the condition of prisoners kept in the interior of Germany was the worst of any men he saw during the war. Some prisoners were kept in France or Holland for recuperation, but not all. Unable to stand the sea crossing to Britain, a few sadly died on board ship, even as their boats drew into harbour. Many more died in hospital, including two of the last -prisoners to be repatriated in March 1919.

From those sick prisoners who came home, there are endless accounts of men turning up unexpectedly on their family's doorstep weighing as little as six stone, walking with the aid of two sticks, their faces gaunt, their eyes staring. This could cause terrible moments of anxiety, especially if a husband, son or brother had been believed long dead. One lady had worn black for two years before her husband arrived home, another attended a memorial service before being reunited with her spouse. Even when a prisoner's return was expected, there was little a family could do to prepare themselves for what they saw. There were cases of mothers not recognising their own sons and wives their husbands. Once the shock had subsided, and adults had come to terms with what they saw, there were the young siblings, many of whom could not help but recoil in horror, unable to get close to brothers, not wanting to be kissed or hugged.

It is debatable how much that mattered to the prisoners, grateful, as they undoubtedly were, to have survived incarceration for up to four years. When perhaps one in ten had died in captivity, most were glad to get their feet back on Britain's shores and to see loved ones again. With two months' POW leave and a small but not insubstantial gratuity to pick up, most prisoners were happy to get out of the army and resume as normal a life as possible. Not all were allowed to leave straight away. Some were merely put through the inconvenience of returning to barracks for a week or two, others were asked to train new recruits or put older ones through their paces. In February 1919, Ernie Stevens was given, of all jobs, that of guarding German prisoners of war at a civilian prison at Lewes in Sussex. It was not until the peace was signed at Versailles that these men were allowed to return to Germany.

The damage done to the prisoners would take years to overcome. Many were so physically incapacitated by their imprisonment that they died at an early age, many never curing the stomach and chest problems that beset them in Germany. An unknown number committed suicide, and many refused to talk about their experiences but displayed odd neuroses that families could only put down to 'that time dad had been a prisoner'. For most, it was simply an inability

175

to see food wasted or a dislike of certain foods such as potato skins or cabbage; for others it was irrational tempers or mood swings, or a desire to be left alone.

The prisoners who came home were left alone, not least by the Government. There had been a huge public clamour for war crimes trials, indeed the first issue discussed, when the Allies met to discuss the terms of the Versailles Peace Treaty in 1919, was the prosecution of war criminals. But while the Government sought the best ways to pursue such men, drawing up lists by the hundred, the prisoners were expected to get on with their own lives, in much the same way as all returning soldiers were obliged to do. Most cared little for the trials, bitter though they were about their treatment in Germany. They had their lives to get on with, or so they thought, though many prisoners were to die within the next ten or twenty years of illnesses that relatives attributed to captivity. That all of these were directly linked to imprisonment is hardly likely, but too many families never had back the same pre-war son, brother, or father, for there not to have been a very strong correlation.

ERNIE STEVENS

Ernie was already in an emotional state when he reached England. He had been away for so long that he was almost nervous about seeing his loved ones again.

As I walked towards home, I stopped at a café. It is very difficult to explain just how much you miss the love of your people and I wanted to collect my thoughts. The lady there welcomed me home and I sat down and had a drink. When I went up to pay, she took the money, then said to me, 'By the way, Ernie, when you get indoors you are going to hear some bad news.'

It was my step-father that opened the door and he shouted

to mum, 'It's Ernie'. I'll never forget that, 'It's Ernie!' So mum came out and of course there was hugging and kissing and then they helped me into the dining room and sat me down and took off my overcoat and my cap, hung them up, and then my mum told me about my half-sister. She had died of influenza, aged 15, and had been buried on Armistice afternoon in Walthamstow Cemetery. That was a blow that really hit very, very hard. I loved that little girl and even now I've got to be very careful I don't cry. Gladys was such a wonderful child. As you can tell, it still hurts.

I mean, I was so glad to get home and to see my step-dad, a man I liked so much. It got to the point, though, that after I'd had something to eat and drink, I asked my mum if she minded if I went out. She was a little reluctant but she nodded and I think she realised that I was not in a fit state to sit there and say almost nothing. It was a very trying time. I had to control myself as much as I could and so one of the best ways was to go out and take a walk up the High Street and try and think things over. At the top of the High Street there was a little gang of about three or four lads and one of them had got hold of the cap of a little boy and threw this kid's cap into the doorway of a shop. I saw red. I must confess I felt like going up and hitting the bully without waiting, but anyway I went up to him and I said, 'Look, what's the idea, go and get that little boy's cap and put it on his head again.' 'Oh, who are you talking to?' he said. I said, 'I'm talking to you, don't you understand?' And then a voice from one of the other boys there said, 'Aye, take it easy, he's been a prisoner of war.'

JACK ROGERS

After arriving at Ripon, Jack had been given a medical check-up, new clothes and a pass to get home. After more than four years he was out of the army.

And that was it, the war for me was over. I arrived home to be met at the door by my mother, my sisters and my young brother. I nearly had a fit, I didn't know what to say. Well, it seemed like coming into a different world, absolutely. It was marvellous to see everyone, my poor father who was a cripple sitting in a chair indoors, oh, it was a moving experience and was for days afterwards. To be home again with them and to be free, I couldn't believe it. I slept for two or three days right off and then of course I had to start a new life.

I don't think the Government cared much about the POWs. I don't think a lot of notice was taken. Anyway, here you were, you were still alive, better than those poor people, many friends of mine, who were dead. Was I angry? I don't think I was feeling that depth about it, to tell you the truth. I was grateful that I was home and able to walk about, still able to work, still living. I was glad to get away from it all. I didn't want to read about it then. I had had four years of war and as a young man, it was a bit too much.

FREDERICK HAMMOND

We landed on December 8th 1918. Oh, the relief, couldn't believe it hardly. We were taken to a Fulham workhouse and they told us if we'd any friends in London or anybody we wanted to get hold of, we could phone. To see my parents again. My father was getting on a bit, he was about eighty then, he'd lost his first wife and married again, so my mother was younger. To see them, after all I'd been through, was lovely.

TOMMY GAY

When the war finished, we were in such poor condition, about seven stone, that I was sent to Holland for convalescence, to a village called Zeevenar just outside the Dutch town of Utrecht where, for six weeks, I was looked after by a lovely family called Bullen. I soon revived and we POWs all got together at Utrecht from where we were taken by Dutch transport to Rotterdam where we, boarded a boat and went to England, going up the Humber and on to Ripon. We were asked many questions, What were we doing? What were they doing to you? Did we resist? We were given a suit of clothes and discharged with a warrant to get home.

When I got home to Peckham they made a hell of a fuss of me, Union Jacks were flying up the street where I used to live. From one bedroom to another, strung across the road was one Union Jack with "Welcome home Tom".

NORMAN COWAN

I arrived at Newcastle with a few soldiers from the area, one afternoon, and after farewells to each other, we went our various ways into civilian life. For myself, I left Newcastle Central Station, then crossed the famous High Level Bridge in Howey's horse-drawn bus into Gateshead, where I swapped to a tram to take me into the Low Fell area, to my parents' place, 46 Haydn Street. We had an upstairs flat and I knocked at the black leaded knocker, but got no answer. There were no balloons for me, nothing, the street was as quiet as a mouse. There was nobody in, so I went round to a back lane that went up to the Old Durham Road, and I tried the back door but it was shut. 'My mum must be out,' I thought. As I turned to walk down the cobbled back lane, I happened to glance up and there was my mother coming down, carrying two bags of groceries. She looked up and she looked at me, laid the bags down and said, 'What d'you think you're doing here?' I said, 'It's the only place I've got, I've come home.' She says, 'Oh well, let's go in and have a cup of tea.' These words of welcome will forever live in my mind and heart. And that was the finish of the Army for me, no celebration, no parties, just a return to home and family. My mother never knew I was even alive, said she'd never received anything, but we didn't speak about it much. She'd taken it for granted that I was dead and now she was glad to get us back. Then the neighbours started coming round, I suppose, I don't recall, but there were no celebrations, nothing. They'd forgotten the war, the civilians, they were fighting each other to gain a job, there were strikes and all sorts. Life had to go on or else I was going to be on the dole, wasn't I, and I decided I wasn't going to be on the dole. I decided that. I went back to the solicitor's office and he said it would be four years before they would put me onto Articles, so I left to find my own way in civilian life.

BILL EASTON

After the fracas in the camp when military discipline had gone too far, Bill was only too glad to be released from duty to get home, grubby though he was.

I had to strip, everything had to be washed, and I put on an old shirt I'd got at home and an old pair of trousers and went out into the garden. A lot of things had changed. My father had remarried shortly before I went abroad and now I had another sister, Sylvie. I asked where she was and my father said she was in bed. 'Wait a minute, I'll bring her to show you.' That was very exciting, having a new two-year-old sister. A lot of people came round to see me over the next few days because I was one of the few that had come back from that business intact. But in truth, I was absolutely bewildered. People would say, 'You're young Bill, aren't you?' and I could hardly answer them. Any amount of lads who had joined with me had been killed, three or four that I personally knew. One chap I knew, Frank Balls, he was a prisoner, and his father kept a very popular pub called The Swan. When I got home, his sister came to see me and asked me about how prisoners were coming out of Germany. I told her I'd come through Holland and said I should think he'd be back very shortly. And do you know, that very day he was running to catch a train somewhere in Germany and he crossed the line and was killed by an oncoming train. I was ever so sorry for her.

CHAPTER TEN

Three Vignettes

This chapter deals with three very different aspects of the prisoner of war experience not necessarily covered in other chapters, but which are nevertheless very important in describing the overall condition of men in Germany.

Whilst researching this book, I received many kind letters from relatives of prisoners. Three stood out and demanded further attention. They were from a child, a grandchild and a daughter-in-law respectively of three former POWs. All the prisoners died many years ago but their stories were equally powerful in entirely different ways. One story is of futility, another of humour and the last of tragedy; each is self-contained, and requires little introduction other than for me to give brief biographical details and a short description of the man each of them portrays.

Two of the prisoners led remarkably parallel, yet contrasting, lives. Born in different parts of the country, into very different households, they were brought up with different attitudes and had markedly different characters. Yet in the First World War, they joined up in the same month and left for France in September 1915, within days of each other. Later that same month, both were captured in the same battle, on or about the same day, in what was their first attack. Later, they shared the same POW camp and, at the Armistice, were repatriated to Britain at about the same time. Over half a century later, they died just a year apart. However, striking though the similarities are, their prisoner of war experiences could not have been more diverse.

The third prisoner was a little older, and fought at different battles. He was traumatised by his experiences and did not survive for long after the war. Haunted by memories of fighting and of his time in a POW camp, he committed suicide in the early 1920s, leaving a wife and two children. His story is told, in part, through the subsequent suffering of his wife, as she fought with heartless authorities for a war pension.

The power of each story stems largely from the accompanying archive photographs and documents. All have been kept as family heirlooms for over ninety years.

ARTHUR HOYLAND, Pte 15364, 10th York and Lancaster Regiment. Born 12th September 1893, died 17th February 1973. Captured at the Battle of Loos, 26th September 1915.

For whatever reason, Arthur Hoyland could not speak to his son about his war experiences, but he did to his grandson. Arthur was a miner all his life, and his grandson saw the injuries his grandfather bore as he undressed for his bath in front of the fire: the deformed thumbs, the whip marks which stood out on his back, the gaping hole in his arm. Afterwards, when Davenports, the local brewery, came round, Arthur would have a few drinks. It would 'loosen him up a bit,' recalled his grandson. 'I found this the best time to ask him about this period in his life.' The stories were not recorded. Kevin, Arthur's grandson, recalls what his grandfather said only from memory. They are tantalising fragments of a fascinating story.

Arthur Hoyland was captured at the Battle of Loos when he acted as a runner, taking messages to a machine gun crew on Hill 70. Wounded in the arm, Arthur stayed with the crew as they fought on until they were overwhelmed, he and a Geordie gunner being the only survivors. Although injured, they were beaten up before being taken back by train to

Germany, travelling three days without food or water, their wounds alive with maggots. They were taken to Rennbahn POW Camp, or Münster II, as it was also known, where Arthur stayed until September 1916. After this, he was sent to Schneidermühl Camp in eastern Germany and then to Aldamm Camp near Stettin. In April 1917, Arthur was moved with a group of men to a notorious work Kommando at Pommerensdorf Chemical Works. On the second day there, Arthur was attacked by two guards, as he later recalled in a sworn deposition given to the British Government. 'I was badly assaulted by Trinke and Neumann who acted like brutes. On the second day, after working all night, Trinke struck me several times on the back and legs with an insulated wire and Neumann jabbed me in the ribs with the butt end of his rifle.' He told how he was assaulted 12 times in the first three weeks while at the Chemical Works, including one incident when 'Trinke was drunk and lined about ninety prisoners (including myself) outside a long hut. He then called all the guards out and ordered them to load their rifles to terrorise us.'

Kevin Hoyland: 'His experiences scarred him mentally, you could see tears in his eyes, you could tell by his face. He slept on the floor for 18 months when he came back, so used was he to sleeping on the ground. His experiences were terrible. They were put to work in a sugar factory where a German sergeant told my grandfather that Kitchener was dead. He asked, 'What will you do now?' and my grandfather replied that he might have sunk Kitchener, 'but not the bloody army'. The German sergeant hit him on the jaw with a rifle butt and knocked him to the ground. He then pushed the bayonet into my grandfather's throat, cutting him on the right side of his neck. A German officer came and stopped what was happening. My grandfather's head was shaved and he was put on bread and water for two weeks.

After this, my grandfather and two others decided to

escape, but all three were captured after a couple of days, being discovered by an Alsatian dog. When they were taken back to the camp, they were hung up by their thumbs and whipped with wire. I know they tried to poison this dog with a sponge coated in fat, but the animal refused to eat it.

Soon after, they were transferred to another camp where they escaped again, but were captured hiding in the ruins of a chimney some four or five miles away. This time my grandfather was put in front of a firing squad, blindfolded, and the order was given to shoot. He heard the firing pin hit the chamber on the rifle, but felt no pain, the guards laughing in amusement.

After this I do not know where he ended up, but it was very cold. They were told if anyone escaped all the others would have their blankets confiscated and that they would freeze to death. They were sent out on working parties with a guard for each group. By this time, the Germans were just as hungry as the prisoners, and while out working they persuaded one guard to shoot a wild stag, which they buried in the snow. Each day they went back to cut a piece of meat, cooking on a makeshift stove with heat provided by candles.'

When Arthur came home, he was just a bag of bones, but he soon recovered and wanted to get on with his life as a miner. Two years later, however, he was called to give evidence at the trial of three Germans in Leipzig, in Germany.

The Leipzig trials, as they were known, were the first international attempt to make unlawful acts of war punishable. Some 3,000 Germans were at first cited by the Allies as war criminals but the list was slowly whittled down so that, of the names put forward by Britain, only four low-ranking Germans were prosecuted. The trials took place in May 1921, two and a half years after the Armistice. By this time, Britain had neither the enthusiasm nor the political will to pursue trials with any vigour. Furthermore, post-war diplomatic manoeuvrings had ensured that it was no longer in Britain's national interest to prosecute Germans accused of war crimes.

The trials were a farce, the longest sentence awarded being just ten months, for gross brutality to prisoners of war. The British contingent that was sent to Germany numbered about 70 in all and included 60 former prisoners called to give evidence. Arthur Hoyland was one of these men.

'My grandfather didn't want to go at all, he'd gone through enough as it was. When he was given notice that his evidence was required at the trials he just ignored it, then one day two officers from Scotland Yard turned up and said he had no choice, he'd have to leave with them. The last thing he wanted to do was to go to Germany but he went and gave evidence, I believe against this man called Neumann. My grandfather was very bitter and told me he could have shot the defendants, saying that they were evil and had taken pleasure in what they had been doing. I know my grandfather was questioned in the witness box and a transcript was made which was given to him but this was lost in a family fire. All I have now are a few documents and his passport which shows that he went back to give evidence, for what that evidence turned out to be worth.'

JULIUS ADAMS, Pte 15775, 7th Northamptonshire Regiment. Born 27th February 1888, died 1974. Captured at the Battle of Loos, 25th September 1915.

Julius Adams' three years in captivity were some of the most creative of his life. He acted, drew, performed in cabarets, and edited the camp magazine. Although he was hungry, often starving, his gifts undoubtedly helped him survive years behind barbed wire, to the extent that he loved to recall those times to his two young sons.

He was captured amid total confusion at the battle of Loos. Julius recalled, some fifty years later, that 'Jerry's methods were quite business-like. They first blew us out of our trench with nicely placed shells, then shot us down as we tried for another one – which happened to contain the people who were shooting at us.' Called to give in before they were wiped out, Julius and the other survivors surrendered. Within days, he was on his way to Germany, where he was taken to Rennbahn Camp on the edge of Münster, a large encampment of huts built on the town racecourse by the prisoners themselves during the winter of 1914/15. He was to stay here for the rest of the war.

'He loved talking about those times, he wasn't one of those who wouldn't speak about what they'd been through,' recalls his son Jonathan Adams. 'When I was a little boy he would often take me for a walk around the park and he would talk to me about the big bombs and so forth. He was starving in the camp and once told me how he had used his finger to clean out the inside of a sardine tin. He also recalled people being covered in lice, but I don't remember him saying that they were ill-treated, rather he told me if any one got smacked around a bit, it was the Russians.'

Julius Adams: 'The camp was arranged in four great blocks with a cook-house and wash troughs in the centre. Believe me, that cookhouse formed the one centre of interest to all, the place being thronged with hungry nosed men who entertained the forlorn hope that some soup would come out. Perhaps it comforted them to be near it.

It is an endeavour to describe existence in a German POW camp of fifty years ago. Fifty years! I sometimes question why time has so exacted his toll from my once robust frame, yet leaving memory green as ever. I have, when the mood takes me, but to close my eyes to relive again scenes indelibly imprinted of people and occurrences in the wire-encompassed world wherein three of the best years of youth were passed – I hesitate to write 'wasted'.

Visions crowd upon each other – pictures of hungry, dejected new arrivals – the eagerly awaited wielding of the soup-ladle by an Italian NCO with a big stick for protection from submersion by his frenzied vociferous soup queue – the pitiful bread ration – the fishy red seal-flesh.

Occasionally, a Russian of an acquisitive turn might secure a few potatoes while a member of a spud-peeling fatigue, with the idea of exchanging with us against German bread.

Modus operandi consisted of peeling a few and popping the next down inside his pants, repeating until a mounting sense of discomfort called for discontinuance of the operation. His trade with the British did not wax, the grey hue of his wares bearing testimony to his prolonged abstinence from soap, and abysmal ignorance of sales presentation.

A POW camp is a small world of mortals isolated from activities pursued under happier conditions, where depravity can gain a foothold, but where also one's character may blossom. When a small gift of food to another might transcend a rich man's largesse.'

Jonathan Adams: 'My father was ideologically a conservative by nature and was very puritanical and often judgmental. But he also had a sense of humour and could play the clown in the camp, which probably saved him, helping him to distance the bad things from himself and perhaps protecting him from attack. He was never anti-German, in fact he learnt a bit of German in classes in the camp as well as a bit of French from a Frenchman who ran a hotel in Cadiz.

My father had been a clerk in an office before the war and when he came back, he worked again as a clerk, this time in a shoe factory. He kept his interest in art and at one time did a few etchings with a press he bought; they were very good. But he wasn't able to be as creative as he had been as a prisoner. He was under a lot of pressure at work and was demoted because he couldn't add up the figures properly, which must have been humiliating. The problem was partly that his wife, my mother, had been sick for a long time and she died just after the war, leaving him to bring up two boys and a girl.

I don't know if he was affected by the war. I didn't notice anything, but as a child you don't. My mother once said to me that when he came back from the war he was a bit peculiar, whatever that meant. It was just something she implied. To my mind, what he went through he romanticised a little, probably more so in later years. Sometimes we would say, 'Oh no, not again, not more about the war,' although now I would love to find out the details.'

ALFRED SCHOFIELD, Corporal 66694, The Machine Gun Corps. Born 4th July 1884, died 23rd February 1922. Captured on the 25th March 1918.

Before the war, Alfred Schofield had worked on the London County Council trams, first as a driver, then later as a conductor. In the nine years before he joined the army, he had worked well and had had only six days off sick, once with a chill, the other time with lumbago. He enlisted on 24th November 1915 but was only called up nine months later on 24th August 1916. After six months' training, he set sail for France in January 1917 and survived fourteen months in the front line before he was captured in the German Spring offensive in March 1918. He was quickly sent to Kassel Camp in Germany and later to Doberitz Camp. At some point, he is believed to have worked in the salt mines. His physical condition was very poor, as the documents below make clear. On the 19th of December 1918, he was repatriated, being demobilised in March the following year. He returned to his old job but could not settle, moving from one job to another. Those who came in contact with him later testified to his clear mental problems. In February 1922 he was killed by a train. He left a wife, Lottie, and two children, Alfred aged 12, and Edna, aged six, all of whom have since died.

The original Inquest Report recorded:

'It is stated in the report that on the 23rd February 1922 the driver of a train reported to the Station Master at Ascot that he had run over a man at Swinley Bridge. The police were informed and deceased's body was found on the railway and conveyed to a neighbouring public house. It is also stated that deceased, who was on a visit to a relative at Maiden's Green, had suffered badly from Neurasthenia.'

The following verdict was returned: 'Killed by a train on the London and South Western Railway while trespassing'.

By all accounts, Alfred was a sensitive man, articulate, with an interest in opera, to which he took his young son. However, his experiences in the war wrecked his mental health. The inquest into Arthur's death maintained that there was insufficient evidence to confirm whether he committed suicide or had died while trespassing. His family was in no doubt: Alfred had committed suicide. His mental illness was such that he often disappeared, members of the family having regularly to walk round London to the homes of various relatives to find him. Very often he wanted to take his young daughter for a walk, but so worried was his wife as to what he might do to himself, that she refused to let him take her.

After Arthur's death, his widow applied to the Government for a pension to help support herself and two children. The application was rejected when documents showed that in February 1919 Arthur had signed that he was not suffering from any disability due to his military service.

The ministry dealing with his case recorded:

'There is no evidence, however, to associate his mental condition with the conditions of his military service and consequently the claim must be rejected on the following grounds.
  1. He did not die as a result of wounds or injuries received in the performance of military duty.

2. He did not die of a disability for which he was removed from duty during his active service, or of which a continuous medical history has been shown from the termination of his active service during the war, and which can be certified to have been attributable to or aggravated by such service.'

The claim had been rejected despite letters from Arthur's post discharge doctor who stated that at the time of death Arthur, 'was under my professional care suffering from Neurasthenia due to war service and is now dead. He came to me twice last February with Neurasthenia and Insomnia. A second note confirmed that 'I last saw this man on 21st February 1922, he was then suffering with Neurasthenia probably due to his late war service.'

An appeal was launched. This time further evidence of Arthur's mental state was supplied, as the documents show.

Another man, a Mr L. Jacoby, stated that he had known Arthur for many years but had recently found him 'very disconnected in many ways when in conversation with him, by which I forward an opinion that he was mentally unbalanced. He seemed unable to give a definite answer to any question put to him, was very erratic, and seemed depressed at times, but at intervals quite normal.'

Lottie Schofield had been left with little money and almost immediately fell out with Arthur's family over who should, or perhaps could, pay for the funeral. In the end, Arthur Schofield was buried with a little girl in an unmarked grave (No 6737) in Tottenham Cemetery on 1st March 1922. His son, Alfred, walked to his father's funeral and in later years recalled to his wife, Rita, how the clergyman had kept stopping the service for the roars of the crowd in the football stadium nearby.

Rita Schofield was born the year Arthur died. She remembers stories about how Lottie had 'fought like a tigress' to keep her family together. 'She took a job as a cashier at the local funfair, and later opened a boarding house to make ends meet. After she fell out with Arthur's family she didn't speak about her husband, the subject became a closed book. Years later she came out to see Alfred and I, who were living in Margate, and she decided she would leave London and start a new life there. She never married again, although she did have boyfriends. She died in 1962 aged in her eighties'.

Edna rarely spoke about her father as she only had the vaguest memories of him. Alfred spoke more. He understood and accepted his father's problems and after Arthur's death, Alfred took over the reins, giving his little sister pocket money and, at 14, taking a job as a barber's boy to learn a trade. Later he set up his own business in his mother's front room, then, when he was 28, he bought his own hairdressing salon where he continued to work until his death.

CHAPTER ELEVEN

Final Thoughts

ERNIE STEVENS

I knew that coming home was not easy. Prisoners had to do the best they could and get on with their lives and not make too much fuss about things. But that week was a terrible week for me. Well, I felt that if anybody upset me, they were in for trouble. I mean the fact that one is released is not easy, coming back to a new world. When you're a prisoner you get used to certainty, you get up and you go to work at a factory, but coming home you don't know what you're going to face. As far as POWs were concerned, we were all given a two months' pass and I think that was a wise decision by the authorities, instead of having these men fiddling around in barracks.

GEORGE GADSBY

I had only received eight parcels of foodstuffs out of the 70 that had been sent. I did not receive any of these until September, parcels of clothing and boots were also sent but never reached me. I never received a single letter or post card from anyone during the whole time I was in captivity and I had no news from my people from the 16th of March until I reached home on the 8th of December.

JACK ROGERS

In my room I've got a letter from the King – King George V – it's in my room now in a frame, in which he and Queen Mary thanked me for all that I'd gone through and for being a prisoner of war, so somebody thanked you for it. I know they couldn't do any more but the recognition was important, that you'd tried your best, and I appreciated that very much. The point is, I've got to be grateful, I'm still here, I'm 106 years old, and I've just had a cup of tea.

FREDERICK HAMMOND

Things used to come out now and again and my family used to say, 'Oh, you've never said anything about that before.' But I didn't want anything to do with the war, I wanted to forget it all. I was glad to get home and never bothered about a war pension. I didn't think the Government owed me anything, in a way, that's why I didn't trouble. But I always said afterwards I was glad in a way that I went.

NORMAN COWAN

We knew they would never make the Germans pay, that any talk was a load of hooey. They asked questions of the prisoners, but then I hadn't been hit. I suppose some fellows would say all sorts of things, but I didn't, I was just glad that I was alive. I suffered something which was beyond hitting. A lack of food to sustain a body, and many were like that, and some succumbed to it, but I managed to get through. I was lucky, I had the opportunity to live again. A fifth of a loaf a day and turnip soup, and whenever I have felt like complaining about food, immediately my mind says – a fifth of a loaf a day and turnip soup.

WALTER HUMPHRYS

I didn't give myself up voluntarily, but better a prisoner of war than being in the trenches. You don't expect to be given chocolates as a POW, but at least you are comparatively safe. You have your life to thank for and you'd rather live your life having a hard time than having no life at all. Nevertheless, you are helpless as a prisoner, and you have to rely on them totally for your bread and water and for the way you are treated.

BILL EASTON

This part of Kings Lynn was like a village then, not built up like it is today. Everyone knew me. People used to speak to me in the street and, to tell you the truth, in the end I got so fed up with congratulations that I didn't go out too much, I was a sort of recluse. In those days I used to do a lot of reading, and that's what I did. But it was a wonderful feeling to be home.

THOMAS SPRIGGS

In 1910 when I lost my father, I went to live with my grand-parents. Grandfather was an estate steward and farmer at Norton Hall on the Daventry/Norton road. I used to love playing, as a thirteen year old boy, in a 40 acre field on a frosty November morning, perhaps with a couple of horses and a single furrow plough, one of my great delights. And I was walking along there, passing this field one day, and suddenly there was a shrill noise and then one bomb dropped, then another one came down and exploded, and then a third. Then I woke up and realised where I was. The noise came from a prisoner of war sleeping in the bunk next to mine and he was snoring to his heart's content – whistle, snore, whistle snore, whistle, snore.